THE
FUTURE
OF BUSINESS

First published in 2021 by Dean Publishing
PO Box 119
Mt. Macedon, Victoria, 3441
Australia
deanpublishing.com

Copyright © Lauren Lowe

All rights reserved. No part of this publication may be reproduced, stored in a retrieval system or transmitted in any way or by any means, electronic, mechanical, photocopying, recording or otherwise, without the prior written permission of the publisher.

Cataloguing-in-Publication Data
National Library of Australia
Title: The Future of Business: How to create a workplace that increases motivation, positivity and happiness
Edition: 1st edn
ISBN: 978-1-925452-38-9
Category: BUSINESS/Entrepreneurship

The views and opinions expressed in this book are those of the author and do not necessarily reflect the official policy or position of any other agency, publisher, organization, employer or company. Assumptions made in the analysis are not reflective of the position of any entity other than the author(s) — and, these views are always subject to change, revision, and rethinking at any time.
The author, publisher or organizations are not to be held responsible for misuse, reuse, recycled and cited and/or uncited copies of content within this book by others.

THE
FUTURE
OF BUSINESS

Lauren Lowe

CONTENTS

INTRODUCTION

Hello and Welcome 8
Foreword 10
How to Read This Book 12
Your Business Journey 13
A Positive Future Starts Here 15

PART ONE: CREATE YOUR CULTURE

Office Culture and Why it Matters 18
Design Your Culture 20
People, Culture and Spaces 22
Understanding What You Stand For 27
How Badly Does Your Office Need a Refresh? 29

PART TWO: DESIGN YOUR ENVIRONMENT

Your Space 36
Plan Before You Do Anything! 47
Space Planning 48
Planning for the Future 52
Furniture Considerations 53
Ergonomics and Productivity 60
Planning for Light and Airflow 64
What to Expect From the Fitout Process 73
Office De-Fit and Make Goods Checklist (Only applicable if leasing) 79
Preparing for a Fitout and Moving Tips 81
Avoiding Additional Costs 84

PART THREE: GROW AND IMPROVE CULTURE

Culture 90
A Sensory Journey 91
Sound 105
Smell 109
Taste 110
Touch 115
Implementing Your Sensory Experience 117

PART FOUR: BUILD SYSTEMS FOR SUCCESS

- The Benefits of S.Y.S.T.E.M.S 124
- Empowering People with Systems: Accountabilities and Reporting 136
- Financial Systems 137
- Recruitment Systems 144
- What Really Drives Employees at Work? 147
- Identifying the Business Need and Hiring New Staff 149
- Mistakes That Business Owners Make During Hiring 154
- Come Join Our Team! 162

PART FIVE: ATTRACT AND RETAIN TALENT

- Our Secret Recruitment System (12 Step Process) 166
- Never Skip a Step! 193
- Setting up for Success 194

PART SIX: CULTIVATE LEADERSHIP AND WELLNESS

- Being a Leader 200
- Showing Love at Work 214
- Random Acts of Kindness 217
- Wellness at Work 220
- Any Excuse to Celebrate! 224
- Become That 1% Business 226
- Giving Back 229
- Never Give Up 232
- Our Own Road to Success 233

Thank You from Lauren 236
Acknowledgements 238
Testimonials 240
Endnotes 243

Hello and Welcome

As co-founder of a reputable Brisbane based commercial fitout company, I wrote this book for two main reasons. One, I wanted to share my knowledge of the fitout process so that you can execute your own fitout with confidence, and my second (perhaps more important) motive, was that I wanted to communicate the ways in which a good workspace can increase motivation, retention, and improve culture. Culture and leadership are a crucial part of any successful business, and enhancing an optimal working environment can create a happy space for you, your employees, and clients.

This is **more than** just a fitout book (even I know that a book on fitouts alone would be *boring*). Whether you are a business owner, manager, leader, or employee wanting to make a difference to your work environment, this book is for you. (I have jam packed it with information for everyone!)

This book is a reference to share lessons and experiences that you can implement in your company. I have included sections on culture, leadership, systems, and recruitment to help you become that 1% business. Let this book guide and inspire you – business can be a hard and lonely road.

As a business owner, mum, and wife, I want to share with you my knowledge and experience, including tips on how to create a great business and the impacts that a well thought out space can have on culture and the team environment. I have also been on both sides of the fitout process. I have delivered to the client, and I have been the client. Because of this, I have a multifaceted understanding of the concerns of a fitout and the benefits of undertaking one. I can assure you that despite the 'mess' of a fitout (the stress, the financial obligations, and everything in between), it is always worth it in the end.

Unfortunately, throughout my career I have been subjected to bullying and harassment. So, I made a promise to myself that when I became a business owner, I would create an environment where people WANT to and LOVE to come to work – a place where everyone feels accepted, respected, safe, and is surrounded by positivity so that we can all achieve together. My passion has always been business – building a team, company culture and leadership (all of which you are about to read about).

My husband, Aaron Lowe and I founded Future Fitouts in 2010. We started small. In fact, we started on our kitchen bench with nothing but an old, second-hand laptop. From the beginning, we had a clear idea of the culture we wanted to create in our business, and I believe that is one part of why our company is successful today. Future Fitouts has been recognised nationally as a recipient of various awards and was featured on Foxtel's *Industry Leaders*.[1]

Future Fitouts is a family-owned company. It is a business with a heart! We care. We deliver excellence and give reassurance of quality. When undertaking a fitout, we consider the needs of staff and clients and strive to maintain a happy environment throughout the process. Our vision is to "change the world by transforming spaces!"

What is the secret to success? By reading this book you will learn that building a reputable company takes more than just time, hard work, sacrifice and dedication. Your team, culture, environment, systems, and leadership all play an equally important part. Invest in your team – your staff are your greatest asset (or biggest liability). As you will discover by reading this book, valuing your employees is a huge part of any company's success.

We certainly did not achieve success on our own. A heartfelt thank you to everyone who has guided us along our journey: mentors, coaches, advisors, and of course, the dedication of every past, present (and future) employee. Thank you from the bottom of my heart.

I am grateful that this book has made it into your hands and I wish you a life of success, reward and happiness on your business journey.

Have a wonderful and positive day!

Lauren Lowe

> **"To have it all is to be able to create a happy balance at work and at home."**
> – Lauren Lowe

(As an added bonus (and as part of our culture to give back) for every book that is sold, Future Fitouts will make a donation to non-profit organisation, B1G1. You can read more about B1G1 later in this book!)

Foreword

It is with a heart brimful of joy and honour that I put pen to paper to write a few indelible words on *The Future of Business*. From the sequestered enclosure of my home office, I recall some pleasant experiences of how I came to know the amiable, successful and humble Industry Leader, Lauren Lowe. It was during the course of my business peregrinations in Q1, 2019 that our paths first crossed.

I was producing and directing a television program that showcased the success stories of Australian businesses across the country and how they came to be. Future Fitouts happened to be one of the stories we were covering at the time. When we arrived at the Future Fitouts offices in Brisbane, the entire workspace – from the entrance and reception area, down to the offices, common spaces and tea rooms – had been carefully organised in such a manner that it felt like home. It was awe inspiring to be there. Each and every piece of furniture or item had been thoughtfully chosen and perfectly placed. Upon the glass coffee table at reception was a light box inscribed with a special message to us (though inconsequential as it may seem, it was extremely powerful, such that it left a long-lasting impression in my heart till this day). It read, "Welcome Annex." Those words were so delightful and made us feel very special.

As our cameras started rolling and we began to capture the story of Future Fitouts on television, Lauren's demeanour was relaxed, warm, sincere and introspective. She spoke with clarity and focus, such that conveyed a succinct narrative which invariably drove her story home. At the end of the production day, we were left enthralled with the high level of hospitality and convivial reception demonstrated by Future Fitouts and the team. It was clear as a litmus test that a culture of motivation, positivity and happiness at work had been sewn into the fabric of Future Fitouts and its workspace.

The *Future of Business* is more than a book. It is the perfect juxtaposition of sacrifice and reward adorned by personal experiences. It is a canvas used as a backdrop to illustrate the careful planning and positioning within the workspace to achieve greatness in business. It is undebatable that business can be challenging – it is perhaps one of the ultimate tests of character and perseverance we can face in our lifetime. Therefore, it is imperative to take notice of the space around us and its direct and/or indirect impact on us, our team and overall business success. It underpins all that we do, from building the right systems to attracting the right people and retaining talent – it all begins with the right foundation and leadership in the right space. The success of your business and team culture will be hinged on the framework of your workspace and positioning (the idea to begin with the end in mind holds true according to Stephen Covey's 7 Habits of Highly Effective People). Our space, culture, people, and environment are all crucial points hammered upon and buttressed throughout this book.

The *Future of Business* could not have come at a better time. It encapsulates the very foundation and essence of every successful business, to which we must all heed. Our economy has undergone yet another metamorphosis which has presented a new set of challenges for business owners around the world. Whether you are working from home, re-entering the commercial space, resuscitating a business swept into hypoxia, or starting a new one from scratch, new ideas shall rise to the surface of your mind as you read this book. It exudes invaluable wisdom that will avail you the temerity to rethink the workspace in relation to future proofing your business and positioning for ultimate success.

To become part of the 1% you must transcend the archaic workspace into a modern and contemporary space, not only for your success, but for your own mental health and wellbeing. Conversely, it is no longer a business, it is a modus vivendi in which our space determines our future in business. It is upon this bedrock that The *Future of Business* is born.

McDonald Emiantor

Managing Director, Annex Media

How to Read This Book

As a business owner, I understand that it is sometimes difficult to find five spare minutes in the day. So, I have designed this book so it can be used as a reference.

You don't need to read this book cover to cover (though I would love it if you did). Take your time. Open it up to a random page, or search for something that interests you. Use this book to your advantage.

Now, sit back, relax and enjoy!

Interactive

Throughout the book, you will notice this symbol. This symbol is connected to the interactive book which is filled with additional information, an interactive approach to understanding layout and fitout, how to videos, tours, before and after transformations and so much more. To have the best experience from this book, I suggest you check it out.

    As a business leader, I believe we should all be equipped with the latest, most up-to-date information. The interactive book will be updated with new material as it becomes available. It is a great way to step into the 21st century of reading and interacting with texts. Take your time perusing it, and keep checking in for updates.

Lauren is sharing more in her INTERACTIVE book.

See exclusive videos, audios and photos.

DOWNLOAD it now at deanpublishing.com/futureofbusiness

THE UNIQUE BUSINESS JOURNEY

Your Business Journey

WHERE ARE YOU NOW?

In a perfect world, business would be simple. Staff would follow instructions, clients would pay bills on time, and sales would just…*happen*. Unfortunately, we are not in a perfect world and business is not so easy (if only!).

Regardless of your business journey – whether you are a sole trader, have just a few employees, or are managing a diverse team across the country – this book will have something for you.

If I could bottle the 'perfect formula' to grow a positive and successful business, the key components would be:

1. **Create. CULTURE**

   o   Design the culture you want

   o   Embed culture from the top down

   o   Cultivate culture within the whole team

2. **Understand why culture is important Design. ENVIRONMENT**

   o   Find the best environment

   o   Create the perfect space

- Appreciate the fitout process and the impact environment has on culture and happiness

3. Grow. CULTURE

- Cultivate culture within the whole team
- Introduce a sensory journey into your space
- Respect the little things that have big and lasting impacts

4. Build. SYSTEMS

- Learn how S.Y.S.T.E.M.S will "**S**ave **Y**our **S**elf **T**ime **E**nergy **M**oney and **S**tress"
- Create systems for growth and consistency
- Systemise EVERYTHING from recruitment to financial and everything in between

5. Attract & Retain. TALENT

- Hire the right people
- Attract world class talent
- Unlock recruitment systems

6. Cultivate. LEADERSHIP

- Be that 1% of business
- Keep your team happy, engaged and motivated
- Retain staff long term

All of this will be explored in detail throughout the six sections of this book so that you can advance your knowledge, move forward, implement quick wins into your business and ultimately create long-term success!

WHERE ARE YOU ON YOUR BUSINESS JOURNEY?

Do you have any burning questions? Check whether any of the below statements apply to you so that you can jump straight to the answers! Otherwise, just keep reading through the entire book!

- ✓ I am not sure what culture is, or why it is important. Turn to page 18

- ✓ I am about to embark on the fitout process, but don't know where to start. Turn to page 47

- ✓ I am looking for some creative ideas around how I can reflect the culture of my business in the office fitout. Turn to page 90

- ✓ I want to start implementing new systems in my business, but I'm not sure how to do this. Turn to page 122

- ✓ My business has a high turnover of staff but I have no idea where my recruitment processes are going wrong. Turn to page 164

- ✓ I need some inspiration on how I can better show my employees that they are appreciated at work. Turn to page 218

- ✓ I want my business to give back to the community, but I have no idea where to find a cause. Turn to page 229

A Positive Future Starts Here

This book is written from firsthand experience based on strategies that have worked for our company, Future Fitouts. By adopting these techniques and practices, our business evolved into a sustainable and profitable award-winning company that now attracts world-class talent, gives back to the community, and is bursting with positivity.

By sharing our journey with you, you too will be able to create a happy and uplifting workplace, filled with a motivated team.

Let me help you realise your workplace's full potential and become that 1% business!

PART ONE

CREATE YOUR CULTURE

(The future is positive!)

> *Clients do not come first. Employees come first.
> If you take care of your employees,
> they will take care of the clients."*
> *– Richard Branson*

Office Culture and Why it Matters

WHAT EVERY BUSINESS OWNER NEEDS TO KNOW!

Believe it or not, on average, work makes up the second largest activity for a human being across their lifetime.

According to Huffington Post Australia, we spend (on average) over 13 solid years[1] at work. Looking at this in another way, the average person will accrue approximately 90,000 hours of work over their lifetime (based on a 40-hour work week, over a 50 year period). This means that the average worker spends around 30% (just under one third) of their total waking hours at work!

I believe that this statistic is higher. Due to the accessibility of technology, we can send and receive emails without moving from the couch and can have any information we want at our fingertips. Many of us also have a Fear of Missing Out (FOMO) if we don't regularly check our social media pages, react to every notification and keep up with what's going on in the world. Checking work emails after hours has become the norm, and is an expectation in some companies. This means more time spent thinking about work and working outside of allocated hours.

Technology and economic conditions have fostered great opportunities for businesses and advancements within industries. However, this has not come without challenges.

Technology has created more local (and global) competition, increased the average number of work hours in a standard week, and shifted work arrangements to include more flexibility, such as working from home or remotely. We are technically always on call, and staff are less concerned with job security (or a 'job for life' mentality) and are more willing to try out multiple careers and different employers across their working life.

WHAT DOES THIS MEAN FOR COMPANIES, LEADERS, AND MANAGERS?

- Constant deadlines
- More competition
- More information
- Higher staff turnover
- More challenges
- The need to create systems

On average, people in Australia change jobs every 3.3 years!

It is getting harder to offer that point of difference so that people want to stay and be a part of something bigger.

With all of this going on, how do you become a business with committed and high performing individuals?

These days, the 'golden handshake' or 'golden watch' is almost obsolete. It does not exist in most companies as staff no longer settle in one workplace for the long haul.

Ask any business owner or manager what their number one stress is. The most likely answer will be, "staff." Why is this? If staff are considered our best asset, how can they also be our biggest stressor?

The constant struggle to meet staff expectations, hire the right people and remove the toxic ones can be a drawn out and costly process. Then, when you finally have it right, a key performing team member resigns and you are back to square one! It's enough to make even the most relaxed business owner break out in a cold sweat!

How can you do it differently? Keep reading!

Throughout the pages of this book will be quick fixes and long-term strategies you can implement to create the culture you want, in the environment you desire, with the people you need.

WHAT DOES ENVIRONMENT HAVE TO DO WITH OFFICE AND CULTURE?

Your chances of growing a successful business will be increased if it is filled with people who want to be there, so it makes sense to create a work environment where people feel comfortable, happy, and motivated. By focusing your time and allocating a budget towards building a positive environment for your team, you will reap the rewards tenfold. After all, a business is only as successful as the people in it, and you want to make sure your team is filled with people who are striving to make your business flourish.

So, let us begin designing your culture.

This step is probably the most complex of the entire journey.

Design Your Culture

Think about the culture you want before you even start to think about a fitout.

Whether you like it or not, culture already exists within your workplace. Depending on the size of the team or years in business, culture can either be changed very quickly – sometimes as simple as removing a single person – or can be a drawn out recruitment and fitout process. Good, bad, or otherwise, culture is already in your organisation.

WHAT IS CULTURE?

Culture is a broad concept that can be defined in a number of ways. When I discuss culture, I am generally referring to the identity or *feel* of a particular business that you can't really explain. This identity can be made up of the vision, mission, values and attitudes that have been defined and indoctrinated by the business owners and have trickled down through to the staff. Culture can also be created through individual team members' personalities. The culture of an office is reflected in the day-to-day operation of the business and through the actions and performance of its management and employees.

Culture can change over time, particularly as the business matures or more team members are brought onboard.

NO ONE CAN DESIGN A CULTURE FOR YOU
Unfortunately, you can't buy a box of 'culture' and implement it overnight, nor can you hire a professional to build the culture you desire. Culture is cultivated from within. It is embedded in the DNA of the company and its founders and is fostered by the team. If you get the culture right and nurture it from the beginning, then you will reap the benefits for years to come.

DON'T KNOW WHERE TO START?
It is important that you put proper thought into the culture you want to create in your business. You can start by answering the simple questions listed below.

- Have you ever sat down and thought about your company culture?
- What do you love and hate about the current culture?
- Has a culture been created without you realising?
- What sort of people do you want to attract to your business?
- What sort of environment do you want to create?
- How will people interact and collaborate within the office?
- How will teams be structured and how will they operate to benefit the business?

Once you have a basic idea of what you want your culture to look and feel like, you will be able to start brainstorming and implementing ways that you can cultivate it.

> ❝ *Culture is POWER,*
> *and Culture is EVERYTHING."*
> *– Tristan White*[2]

People, Culture and Spaces

PEOPLE

Sometimes, culture is formed organically. Other times, careful planning has been put in place so that only certain types of people are attracted to an organisation.

Culture is not about discriminating, it is about being so in tune with your business that you know some people will just not 'fit'. Knowing that your company is not right for everyone is a big step towards designing and maintaining your culture. By retaining only those who strive to uphold your vision and values, you will be able to protect your culture and brand.

I love when a potential candidate comes back after an interview and says, "I just don't feel that this company is right for me." *Winning!* I honestly do everything I can to convince candidates that Future Fitouts may not be right for them. At the end of the day, I am looking for a certain type of person – someone willing to commit to us for the long haul, not just until a better option becomes available. It is much better that the individual acknowledges that they are not the right fit at the recruitment stage, saving both parties time and money.

If you notice that someone is not going to 'fit' or 'gel' with your company during the recruitment or probation stage, it is not the end of the world (it is actually a good thing). Convince them it might not be the right place for them and they may not be happy if they stay. Or, if they have come to that realisation on their own, thank them for their honesty (well done to you for creating a culture where those difficult conversations can be had with transparency). I understand that not everyone will fit in with our company culture and I'm okay with that.

Boost Juice founder, Janine Allis, has designed and preserved a distinct culture within her company and across the Boost Juice franchise through deliberate hiring and fitout decisions. Boost Juice employees are passionate, young, and motivated, and can

> There is a perfect job for everyone, but this company may not be perfect for you!

be seen dancing to loud music and having fun while they work. Visually, the stores are open and bright, and the staff's uplifting energy is projected onto and absorbed by the customer. Because of this, Boost Juice is now an international success, with countless candidates applying every day.[3]

Google is another great example of a company that has used culture to attract and retain the right people. Google has TWO to THREE MILLION applications EVERY year[4] due to its creative, fun, and supportive culture. People want to be a part of something bigger!

Companies like Boost Juice and Google (amongst many others) are not relying on the traditional means of posting job advertisements online and waiting for the 'right' people to apply. They are receiving applications daily, from the best of the best. Imagine having your pick of the finest five-star talent every time you needed a position filled! That is the power of culture. (See Part Four, page 122 for more on recruitment.)

RECRUITERS

Using recruiters is never my first choice. There might be some great ones out there, but unless you are clear on your culture, how can you expect a recruiter to find the right person to match your company?

I receive numerous calls and emails from recruiters every week. You have probably received your fair share as well. Usually, they will take a sales pitch approach with a generic script that starts with something like, "I have this *great* candidate that will be perfect for your business." Now, how on earth could a cold calling recruiter know that a candidate is 'perfect' for our business, when they have never stepped into our office, let alone tried to understand our company culture?

To attract and retain the right talent, we rely on our own rigorous recruitment process. The (very few) recruiters we work with know our culture inside out and have been immersed or inducted into it.

SPACES

People play a big part in creating and maintaining a company's culture, but having the right space for them to do it in is just as important. By taking the time to design a positive and productive environment, you will be surrounded by people who want to come to work every day to be a part of something special.

As you can imagine, the Future Fitouts office is not a standard professional or corporate space. It is bright, colourful, motivating and fun (we knew a good fitout company). Our brief during the design phase was to create a 'Google inspired office' that could showcase what we do and reflect our culture. As a team, we exercise together, share personal stories, and participate in group meditations. So, we needed a space that could facilitate all of those things! We know that not everyone will fit into this culture or enjoy being a part of it. The ones that do, thrive in their positions and love coming to work.

Take a look around your office. Think about what kind of areas you would like to create and how those areas would be used. Do you have a space that could be transformed into a fun and loud zone? Is there an unused corner that could be a designated quiet and contemplative area?

Would your team benefit from having any of these spaces incorporated into the environment?

- Collaborative spaces
- Planning spaces
- Mindfulness spaces
- Quiet spaces
- Eating and socialising spaces

LAYOUT

The layout of furniture and office equipment is an important consideration that many business owners overlook. Think about how the layout of workstations and desks meets your company's goals and promotes the culture you are trying to create. Is the arrangement of furniture promoting teamwork? Or, are the desks positioned in a way that encourages individuals to work independently? There is no right or wrong layout, but it should be designed to reflect how you want the team members to interact. (See Part Two, page 34 for more on layouts.)

Be strategic in the way you seat your staff. People usually tend to speak and bond with those who are sitting next to them and behind them, not across from them. Keep this in mind when you are planning seating for your office space and consider which team members you would like to forge a relationship. However, keep in mind that even the right layout cannot enforce a personable relationship.

If you look at the diagram below, you will notice that the two desks are placed side by side. In a seating plan such as this, it is likely that the people from Team 1 and Team 2 who have their backs to each other will organically form personable relationships and possibly even close friendships. This is indicated by the middle box.

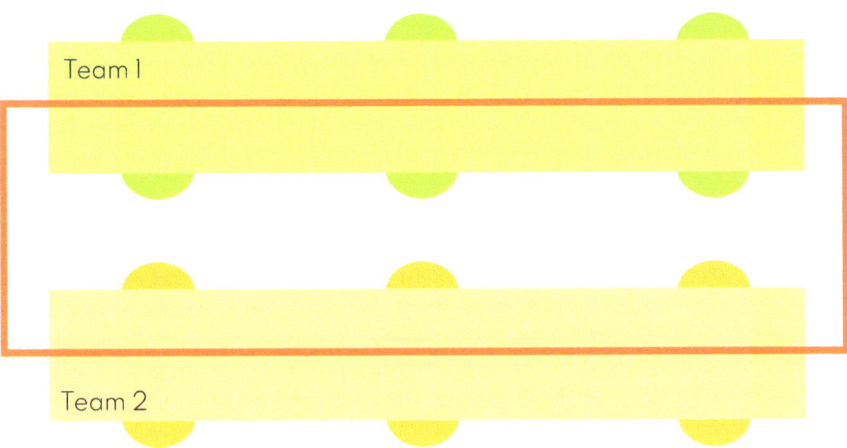

The layout and positioning of your office should also reflect the working styles of different personalities. For example, at Future Fitouts, the quiet workers are placed together, as are the social workers. We have assigned these groups to separate ends of the office to minimise distractions and interruptions.

OPEN PLAN ENVIRONMENTS

Open plan offices can be a double edged sword. If your goal is to create a culture that encourages communication, collaboration, and creativity in the workplace, then open plan is a great design choice for your business. However, if your team requires privacy, or is easily distracted by noise, then this type of office might not be for you. (I *definitely* prefer an open office space, but can appreciate the downfalls of not being able to get deep and uninterrupted work done.)

If you are considering using an open plan layout, you should list the pros and cons of how this type of office will (or will not) work for your specific business and the culture you want to create. You can then explore ways that you can minimise noise and control disruptions. This could include scheduling an hour of 'concentration time' every day where the entire team goes into deep work mode, or using a hat or a sign to signal when someone needs to concentrate and not be interrupted. There are also many design options that you can incorporate into your fitout that will reduce noise pollution (see Part Two for more on this).

TIPS AND QUESTIONS TO CONSIDER WHEN 'DESIGNING YOUR CULTURE'

- ✓ Stand for something 'bigger' that people want to be a part of.

- ✓ Have a clear vision, mission, and values.

- ✓ Design your office to suit and encourage the culture you want.

- ✓ Think about the different personalities within your teams and where they should be situated.

- ✓ Is the seating arrangement (current or future) conducive to the work they are doing?

- ✓ Where do teams sit and how is teamwork dealt with?

- ✓ Are there staff who require privacy or deal with confidential phone calls?

- ✓ Does your office use individual offices or open plan spaces?

- ✓ Is flexible seating, like hot desking or sit and stand desks, something that would be of benefit?

- ✓ How and where does the team collaborate?

- ✓ Are there designated independent quiet working zones?

FLEXIBLE ENVIRONMENTS

Recently, there has been a movement of 'hot desking' or more flexible workspaces, where no one has an individual desk. Instead, staff choose a location to work from each day and pack up any personal belongings each night. Some companies operate on a 'first in best dressed' scenario. While this can work for some organisations (and certainly keeps offices looking tidy), I think it takes away from the personal touch that employees create by having their own desks.

Understanding What You Stand For

YOUR BRAND, VISION, MISSION AND VALUES

The Future Fitouts vision is to **change the world by transforming spaces** and is comprised of two key philosophies.

A. We are transforming spaces to create the foundation for other businesses to succeed.

B. We are a company that gives back and is ultimately changing the world through every fitout we complete.

Our work environment has been designed around this and incorporates our values, brand, goals, and culture.

Creating the right space that suits your brand and is aligned with your vision and values is like laying the foundations of a house.

Make sure you have your vision, mission, and values clear when you begin building or modifying your space. This will assist in creating (or changing) your culture and ultimately the environment in which your business operates.

It is crucial that everybody in your company understands what you stand for. It is a good idea to have your mission statement and values listed or displayed somewhere in plain sight at the office so that everybody can be reminded each day of their importance.

For us, our vision, mission and values are not a corporate policy document that gets shelved and dusted off every once in a while. They guide every business decision we make. From recruitment and strategy planning, to when and how to make difficult decisions, our vision leads us through the good times and bad so that we can achieve something bigger together.

FUTURE FITOUTS™
transforming your commercial space

VALUE STATEMENTS

CHANGING THE WORLD BY TRANSFORMING SPACES

TAKE OWNERSHIP. Be accountable for your actions and responsible for the outcome
- ☐ I take ownership and pride in my work, I set my standards high
- ☐ I am responsible for my actions and accountable for the outcomes
- ☐ I deliver consistently and produce quality results
- ☐ I carry out my duties in a professional, diligent and responsible manner

DISPLAY LEADERSHIP. Motivate self and others to succeed and make it happen!
- ☐ I show initiative and motivate myself and others while performing my duties
- ☐ I share my knowledge, inspire others to achieve and listen to ideas from others
- ☐ I make it happen, lead by example for others to follow and exceed expectations
- ☐ I am a team player and offer, seek and accept assistance when required

BRING YOUR BEST SELF! Authentic, genuine and honest
- ☐ I bring the best possible version of myself everyday
- ☐ I am authentic, I am genuine and I am honest with myself and my team (even when the truth is hard)
- ☐ I maintain a high level of open and honest communication and communicate my inability to keep an agreement at the first available opportunity
- ☐ I accept and offer constructive feedback, am reliable and only make agreements I intend to keep

CREATE WOW! Everyday moments of positive surprises
- ☐ I look for moments to create positive 'wow' reactions amongst my team and clients
- ☐ I share a passion for learning and initiate change to do things better
- ☐ I see the positive in every situation
- ☐ I seek opportunities to do more with less, master the power of leverage

CHOOSE YOUR ATTITUDE. Find something to be grateful for
- ☐ I maintain a positive, fun and happy attitude in the workplace
- ☐ I choose my reaction to situations and find things to be grateful for
- ☐ I respect myself and treat others with the same level of courtesy and respect they deserve
- ☐ I show integrity and avoid situations that may cause conflict of interest

Work safe. Go home safe
- ☐ I understand the "Future Fitouts Way" and our commitment to WHS, Quality and Environmental Policies
- ☐ I comply with all Future Fitouts policies, procedures and work instructions and relevant legislative requirements
- ☐ I maintain accurate records
- ☐ I look after myself and my colleagues

Name .... Signature .... Date ....

© Copyright March 2017

In addition, a detailed copy of our value statements is signed and presented in a frame to every team member during onboarding and is then displayed on each individual's desk. Our values are also proudly displayed across the walls of our office.

Refer to my interactive book for photos!

If you want to learn more about vision, mission and values, I recommend reading the book *Culture is Everything*[5] by Tristan White (just wait until you finish this one!). It will provide you with valuable insights into how you can create a stronger culture in your workplace.

How Badly Does Your Office Need a Refresh?

It can be difficult to recognise if an upgrade or refurbishment is needed when you are working in the same space, day in and day out. We become so absorbed in our jobs that we do not really take notice of what is happening (or falling down) around us.

To help, I have compiled a list of ways to help you decide whether it is time to reboot the office, and give it a refreshing new look and feel.

1. You are struggling to keep up with clients

This can become daunting. You know the need is rising fast, but you are trying to make do with what you have.

In this rapidly changing world, it is important to keep up to date with new technologies so that you do not lose business. Choose to embrace new systems and technology and get educated on what you need to do (and acquire) to keep up with the current and new clients coming in. Get the training you need and upgrade your equipment. Hire a professional if you have to. You want to welcome new business in, not turn it away.

2. **Your office belongs in the 1950s (even the 1980s is considered dated)**

This is *fine* if you are going for the 1950s look (think old style diners). However, if you are not running a mid-century themed restaurant, then it is time for an upgrade.

People buy with their eyes first. If they are impressed when they walk into your office, you will be more likely to keep them as a client. This also applies to staff. You want to keep your employees happy so that they stay with you and remain loyal to your business. Once you update and freshen up the surroundings, you will experience boosted morale all around the office.

As mentioned above, you want to stay up to date with the latest technology. These days, bulky fax machines and big photocopiers are not necessary (unless you run a printing company). Look at what can be upgraded and explore your options. Seek assistance from a professional if need be.

3. **Your staff have low morale**

The wellbeing of your staff should always be a priority. Nobody wants to work in a cluttered, dirty, or out of date environment. Spruce up the office, add some colour, and create better spaces.

Take the time to create a better working environment so that your staff actually *want* to come to work and feel happy in the office. You will find that employees will produce better outcomes if they are happy and comfortable. When you begin to plan the refurbishment, allow the staff to have some input, as this will increase morale and respect within the office.

4. **The office is bursting at the seams**

If the office is too crowded then it is time to move! Be strategic in this relocation and use the time to create a truly perfect (or near perfect) environment. Remember, you are not alone. This is the time to bring in the experts who can drive the project with your ideas in mind.

At Future Fitouts, we are with our clients the whole way, and never allow them to feel overwhelmed or frustrated. Transparency is important, so we make sure we communicate exactly what we are doing during each stage of the fitout process. Do your research and find the right company for you.

5. **Your business doesn't shine**

If your office space is not reflecting what your values are, then it is time for a refresh, a reboot, or a refurbishment. Your office should reflect the personality of the business, your brand, and what you stand for. It should accurately depict the business and what it does. If it does not do all of these things, then you know it is time for a change. There are many ways to incorporate branding and have it reflected throughout a space. Sometimes, just adding a splash of colour here or there or a picture of a quote may be all that is needed in the short term while you plan the big fitout event.

By having an up to date and edgy space that reflects your company, you will be more likely to keep staff happy, attract new business through the door, and achieve more than you ever thought possible.

QUIZ TIME

Let's take a quick quiz to see whether your office needs a refresh.

Tick those statements that apply to your space.

- ❏ My space uses demountable partitioning.
- ❏ Fixed workstation screens block some (or all) of the natural light in my space and creates a closed off feeling.
- ❏ There are no plants in my space.
- ❏ The wall paint is peeling.
- ❏ The wall paint is a dull shade.
- ❏ The carpet is worn.
- ❏ The ceiling has sagging tiles or has been affected by water damage.
- ❏ The furniture is dated.
- ❏ The colour scheme is dark.
- ❏ There is no clear layout in my space and the staff feel like they are working on top of each other.
- ❏ The location of workers and teams does not promote communication channels.
- ❏ The furniture is mismatched and has no connection or flow.
- ❏ The staff complain about the old toilets, small kitchen, or unpleasant environment.

Add up your score _____

Your total will tell you how dire your fitout situation is!

One to four points: Hope is not lost! But, it does sound like your space could benefit from a refresh. Have you considered changing up the layout of your space, or incorporating some simple accessories, like plants or artwork, to liven things up? Read on to discover what other small touches you can add to give your space the pick up it needs (and deserves)!

Five to eight points: Eek! It sounds like your space needs a serious makeover. Are you able to make these improvements yourself? If not, it might be worth engaging a design or fitout company to help you make your office really shine. Keep reading to find handy DIY tips-and-tricks that will really make your space pop, as well as what to look for in a fitout company before engaging one.

Nine to 13 points: Your space *definitely* needs a fitout! Is your current office able to accommodate your growing business needs, or will you have to move buildings? Get planning and call your fitout company ASAP! Follow our checklists when considering a new office space, and embarking on the moving and fitout process (see Part Two, page 34 of this book).

PART TWO

DESIGN YOUR ENVIRONMENT

(There's positivity in the works!)

Your Space

TO OWN OR LEASE?

The decision to lease or own can be a strategic one. I have a biased view that it is better to own property wherever possible (however there are many reasons why leasing can be a better option). Regardless of the choice you make, it is important to be tactical, do your research and get some professional advice if you are stuck.

Some things to consider and assist in making your decision to lease or own a commercial space are outlined below.

OWNING

Owning your building gives you the freedom to be creative with your space. You don't have to worry about lease agreements, and anything that you add to the premises is an investment into your business. There is no risk of being asked to move out, to make good any modifications to the space, and there are no landlord stipulations. However, owning an office space is not always possible. Due to factors like initial outlay and cost, the location where the business operates, and whether the space you really want is even available to purchase, owning a space is not always a viable option.

LEASING

If you are leasing, you have the freedom to move around, test the space, and work the market. You can consider all of this before making a move into something more permanent.

When leasing, look through the agreement and consider any landlord incentives. You may be able to negotiate incentives for your business, including the cost of some (or in lucky cases all) of the fitout! You might also like to negotiate other terms of the lease, including the duration of tenancy and any other clauses you would like to have amended. If in doubt, seek legal advice. Always make sure you know what you are signing before you sign it.

	PROS	CONS
LEASE	o Lower upfront cost so cash flow can be used elsewhere in the business (or towards a fitout). o Tenant is only locked into occupying the premises for the duration of the lease. o Tenant can take on more space in the future if required.	o Landlord may restrict the use of the space. o Landlord may require approval for any changes or alterations to the space. o Tenant may spend money on a fitout that needs to be removed in full before vacating the premises. o Landlord may refuse to renew the lease at the end of the lease term. o Tenant is subject to rent increases.
BUY	o Purchaser owns an asset. o Potential for capital gains. o No landlord restrictions or permission required. o Owner can convert the space internally without landlord approval.	o Higher initial outlay. o High cost of acquisition. o Loss of cash flow for the business. o Business might grow out of the space. o May want to change locations in the future.

KEY CONSIDERATIONS

Keep the below factors front of mind when you are buying or leasing a commercial property.

THE AREA

1. **Location, location, location**

    Unless you are working remotely, this is a big one. You want to provide ease of access to the building for staff and clients. You also want to be able to maximise the exposure of your business through its location.

    Do your research. Find some buildings that you like and hang out there. Check out the foot and road traffic. Can people see your office from the street? Will the location bring interest and potential new clients to your business? Does signage on the building attract cars driving past?

    You should also consider whether your team is 'in and out' all day visiting clients, or if are they based in the office. If there is a majority of 'ins and outs', consider the driving time (or downtime) that it may be costing your business. Time is Money.

    When Aaron and I acquired one of our premises, we spent more than we had allocated in the budget. The building was less than five minutes from most of our projects and close to the CBD. As most of our team is required to work in and out of the office, it was a better business and financial decision for us to spend more on location and have our employees working within five minutes of their clients, rather than purchasing something cheaper in the outer suburbs and doubling the driving downtime.

2. **Amenities and facilities**

    It sounds simple, but think of the type of people you want to attract and have working for your company. Prospective employees will consider the location of your business and nearby amenities before deciding to work for you, or even showing up to an interview.

    What amenities are nearby that will attract the team you want? Are there plenty of food options, transport, and parking? Are there any gyms in the area that may offer lunch time classes? Or, is your only option the local smoko shop in the middle of nowhere with a day-old chicko roll in the bain marie? (A bit exaggerated, but you get my drift!)

3. Do you require parking for staff and/or clients?

Does anyone in your team require a parking space? Do clients visit your office, or are all meetings conducted offsite?

Have you ever looked at using a business located in the inner city but thought it might be easier to go somewhere based in the suburbs, because access is easier? If clients are visiting and parking is unavailable or very costly (like CBD locations) this may deter them from choosing your service. You don't want to lose potential clients over a lack of parking. This needs to be considered when deciding on the right location for your business.

THE SPACE ITSELF

4. Is there enough room for future growth?

It is great to have your own property. However, when considering buildings, look at the size of the space and whether there is ample room to grow. Sometimes, it is better to buy a larger space and sublet part of the area out. When you are ready to expand, you can just extend into the previously subleased areas, rather than having to move to a different building and complete a whole new fitout.

Think about your future business plans, staff numbers, boardroom and meeting room sizes, and the amount of restrooms. Compare various spaces and do your research!

5. Make a list

Making a list of what you want in a space is useful before you go out and look for one. There should be specific things on your list such as toilets, kitchen amenities, separate offices – whatever you need. Then, add the 'non-negotiable' items. These are essentials that the space *must* have, and will contribute to the culture you are creating. Be prepared before you start looking and accept that the list may change many times as you get clearer about what you want.

6. The actual fitout

The fitout is the first impression made on potential and existing clients, and of course, your staff.

Any custom joinery and furniture should reflect the culture of your business and the atmosphere you want to create. You would not install cheap flooring in a high-class business! These little things are important and can make a big impact. (More on fitout later in this section.)

Our office building choice was very strategic! We acquired a property located in a high profile area with lots of traffic and street exposure. Our brand is constantly on display (the neon lights at night really help). The location is close to amenities in the location we wanted to do business (to attract the right team members) and is recognised on Google maps. The building has plenty of parking options for clients and the space itself is the right size to allow for future expansion.

While it was more than we originally wanted to spend, we considered all of these factors from a future business viewpoint and decided it was a very worthwhile investment for our business!

TIP!

Did you know?
Most people are unaware that you can actually depreciate the cost of the fitout. Some of the costs associated with a fitout (whether you own or rent) is tax deductible!

BONUS SECTION

Commercial Property Investment and Depreciation

I love property and am very fortunate that my husband Aaron also shares this passion. I think sometimes we take it for granted how much we know about property (possibly a future book…).

For now, I want to share some of my knowledge with you so that you can make the best possible choice for your situation.

Commercial investing is unlike residential investing, and investors should understand these differences. Investing in commercial property is not the right thing for everyone, so I have compiled some high-level considerations before considering commercial property.

Commercial Investment Considerations

- If you are going to invest in commercial property, you need to understand how this particular market works, how it differs from the residential market, and what its drivers are. In addition to population growth (which is the main driver in the residential market), commercial property is driven by a number of wider economic factors.

- The economy and interest rates impact consumer spending, demand for services, business performance, a tenant's ability to make rental payments, and a landlord's ability to pay back a loan.

- Demographical trends and patterns can affect commercial property and demand. For instance, with the rise of baby boomers making a 'sea change', there is now more demand for healthcare services in areas traditionally considered holiday locations. Similarly, our aging population has driven demand for aged care facilities, while the growing need for childcare services has created competition for property that can be used by these businesses.

- Changing consumer habits (often going hand in hand with evolving technologies) have an impact on the commercial property market. For instance, the rise of online shopping in the past decade has increased the demand for industrial warehouse properties.

- Financial considerations, such as obtaining finance for a commercial property, differs from securing a residential mortgage and is often more complex. Pricing may not be set in stone, and the terms can sometimes be negotiated. Individuals should consider whether a commercial finance structure suits them and their investment goals.

- When buying a commercial asset (from an investor perspective) the value is derived from the tenant or lease in place and the duration or terms of the lease. On the flip side, if the asset is vacant (purchasing as vacant possession), you are buying the future potential to attract a quality grade tenant into the space and generate a return. We have a number of investor clients that we work with to fitout vacant spaces. Their sole outcome is to create a functional space that will attract high-grade tenants to move in immediately.

- Commercial leases are complex, and a number of operating expenses can be passed onto the tenant. Whether you are buying or leasing a commercial space, ensure you understand the terms of the lease and the costs that you will be responsible for.

> ❝ *Claiming depreciation is paramount for commercial property investors. A depreciation claim can provide the difference in income for owners to turn a negative cash flow property into an investment with a positive cash flow."*
> *– Bradley Beer, CEO, BMT Tax Depreciation*

BONUS SECTION

Commercial Property Depreciation

Generally speaking, residential property appreciates or doubles in value every seven to ten years. Commercial property is a little different, as it is the lease and the fitout that usually adds value.

There are three main components to commercial property: the land, the building, and the lease. The building (including fixtures and fittings) depreciates overtime. However, many commercial property owners are unaware that they can claim this depreciation at the end of each financial year. Almost 80% of property owners do not take advantage of this tax incentive and miss out on claiming back thousands of dollars every year. Imagine what that money could do in the long run!

Here is what Bradley Beer suggests to make an informed decision when it comes to investing in your business.

1. **What is depreciation and what can be claimed?**

   The Australian Taxation Office (ATO) requires investors to report any income earned from a commercial property as part of preparing their income tax assessment. Commercial investment property owners are entitled to claim depreciation. Depreciation is a deduction available due to the wear and tear of a building's structure (capital works deduction) and its fixtures and fittings (plant and equipment items) over time. It is considered a non cash deduction, meaning investors do not need to spend any money to be able to claim it.

2. **No property is too old**

   Owners can claim capital works deductions for any commercial property built after 20 July 1982. Despite restrictions the ATO places on capital works deductions based on the construction date of the property, the owner may be entitled to claim any recent renovations which have taken place since 20 July 1982, even if they were completed by a previous owner. Depreciation of plant and equipment items can be claimed regardless of age. Examples of plant and equipment items include carpets, air conditioning units, hot water services, lights and light fittings.

A specialist quantity surveyor will conduct a site inspection to take pictures and make note of additions that have been made to the property and will capture all existing plant and equipment items. They will provide an itemised tax depreciation schedule which outlines all the deductions available for the lifetime of the property (40 years).

If a commercial property owner is thinking of completing a renovation, they should also request their quantity surveyor to complete an inspection before and after the renovation takes place, as any removed items may be entitled to be written off as an immediate deduction.

3. **Depreciation of a fitout**

Working out who is entitled to claim depreciation for certain items can be a complicated process when compiling a property depreciation schedule for commercial buildings. Both owners and tenants have the right to claim depreciation entitlements when it comes to a fitout installed in a property.

Commercial tenants are able to claim depreciation on any fitout they add to a property. These items include assets such as desks, blinds, shelving, carpet, vinyl, fire equipment and security systems. Commercial building owners also may be able to claim depreciation on any easily installed assets and any assets left behind by previous tenants once their tenancy has ceased.

If lease conditions mandate that tenants return a property to its original condition at the end of a tenancy, a specialist quantity surveyor can prepare a depreciation schedule conveying which items are removed or scrapped so these can be written off, escalating the left over value so it can be claimed as a 100% deduction in the year of removal.

4. **Choose a method of claims that works with your investment strategy**

Once depreciation has been calculated, property investors can select from two methods by which to make their depreciation claim. These are called the prime cost and diminishing value methods. The intentions of the property investor can help to determine which depreciation method is most suitable.

Under the diminishing value method, the deduction is calculated as a percentage of the balance you have left to deduct. Under the prime cost method, the deduction for each year is calculated as a percentage of the cost.

The method chosen depends on the long and short term strategy of the property investor. If you claim using the diminishing value method, you are claiming a greater proportion of an asset's cost in the earlier years, thereby increasing deductions earlier. Alternatively, the prime cost method spreads deductions out over time, working well for a longer term investment.

5. **Consult with a specialist quantity surveyor**

Calculating the depreciation for commercial properties can be quite a complex process. For this reason, it is important to consult with a quantity surveyor who specialises in tax depreciation.

The ATO recognises quantity surveyors to be one of the few professionals with the appropriate construction costing skills to calculate the cost of items for depreciation purposes. Quantity surveyors are qualified under Taxation Ruling TR 97/25, and also gain access to the latest ATO rulings and information through their affiliations with industry regulating bodies.

Quantity surveyors work regularly with property managers and accountants to maximise deductions available to property investors. BMT Tax Depreciation completes tens of thousands of depreciation schedules for accountants each year.

How to claim depreciation

Claiming the fitout costs of a commercial property should be easy. At Future Fitouts, we have aligned with BMT to offer our clients discounted and detail specific advice to help them every step of the way.

Both owners and tenants can benefit from claiming depreciation. It is especially important for commercial property owners to take advantage of depreciation deductions, as doing so can make a significant difference to cash flow.

To find out what depreciation deductions are available, the owner should contact a specialist quantity surveyor and ask them to provide a comprehensive depreciation schedule. As part of this process, a depreciation expert will complete a detailed site inspection. They will take measurements, detailed notes and photographs to ensure that the owner receives the maximum claim for the wear and tear of the building and the assets it contains.

An inspection is even more important when a property owner has leased their building to a tenant who has installed a fitout. This is because both the owner and the tenant can simultaneously claim depreciation deductions. The owner can claim deductions on the building structure and any original assets, while the tenant can claim depreciation on any fitout works they carried out during their occupancy.

Some leases contain conditions that direct a tenant return a property to its original state. A tenant would therefore be able to claim any remaining deductions for the cost of items they remove and scrap when they vacate the property.

EXTRA BONUS!

If you become a Future Fitouts client, ask us how you can secure a discount with BMT on the cost of preparing a Depreciation Report

 Check out the interactive book for more on depreciation!

Plan Before You Do Anything!

Before refurbishing your office, moving spaces, or speaking with a fitout company, create a high-level plan. A good fitout company will take you through the entire process, however, it is important to consider everything yourself first.

1. **Concept ideas with culture in mind**

   As previously discussed, it is essential that you consider culture and team interaction when planning your space. Take the time to design this component. Understand where team members will sit, how they will collaborate, and what other spaces are required in your workplace to create the culture you want. Don't worry if you are not a design expert. At this stage, all you will need is a rough layout plan.

2. **Make your lists**

   Start with your 'must have' list. This list will include the *essentials* your business needs in order to succeed. Consider things like the kitchen, boardroom, desks, meeting rooms, and amenities. You can amend this list as necessary.

   Having this list will help give you a clear vision of what the office will look like and how it will operate. It will also allow the fitout company to understand your requirements and create a budget.

3. **Create a board**

   Some people are more visual than others. You may like to create a vision board of what you would like your office to look like. You can choose to play with ideas, like colour schemes and styles at this stage. Use Pinterest or Instagram to find some inspiration online.

4. The dream list

Next, put together your 'dream list'. This can be something that you work towards if money, time, and space permits. What would your space look like in a perfect world? Allow yourself to be extreme and wild with your imagination. You might be able to achieve some of your ideas more easily than you think.

Have a chat with your fitout company or designer about your dream list and see if they can help you achieve it. You may be surprised at what small changes can be made to reduce costs but maintain design integrity.

5. Have a budget

Planning includes having a budget and allowing at least 10% (or more) for contingency. As you work through the fitout process, your budget will become more fixed and accurate. However, even in the initial stage of the fitout, you must have some sort of budget. The last thing you want is to be left with a half-finished office space and no more money! Remember to allow for essential services like electricity, hydraulics, mechanics, and air conditioning. These things can come at a very high cost.

Space Planning

OPEN OR CLOSED OFFICES

When planning your space, consider who will be working within the office and whether an open plan layout will benefit your staff. Think about how your team works (and how you want them to work) and factor that into your design. You can then map out your office layout around the space. A reputable fitout or design company will be able to provide great assistance with this.

> *If you are clear on what you want, the fitout company you engage will be able to price more effectively and bring your dreams to reality.*

When like-minded employees who share the same goals, tasks and clients are in the same environment together, it boosts productivity in the workplace. However, an open plan space may not be ideal for those teams who need privacy or quiet spaces to get their work done.

Improving the flow of your office with departments, rooms, and thoroughfares laid out logically and efficiently will also reduce frustrations and improve the function of the whole office.

HOT DESKING

Are you creating a space that makes individuals to feel at home, or do you want an office where everyone packs up their desk at the end of the day? Depending on the culture you want to create, the choices are endless.

You may choose to designate an area purely to hot desking and allow other professionals to come in and work in your office. Or, you might want to create a space where your employees have the freedom to decorate their desks however they choose. This all needs to be considered in the planning stage of the process.

BREAK OUT ZONES, FUN AREAS, AND QUIET TIME

If you are trying to stimulate a culture of positivity, healthy mindset, and office wellbeing, you might like to include breakout zones and quiet areas in your office plan. Look out for unused corners and spaces that can be transformed into useful communal areas.

Does your company promote having fun at work? Consider including a tennis table or pinball machine in the office! Keeping an open mind about shared spaces will allow you to be more creative with your office design.

MIXED USE SPACES

Mixed use spaces are a great way to save on space and have a multifunctional area. The boardroom could double up as a yoga room, or the small meeting room could also function as a meditation or quiet space. If you do not have enough room to dedicate a separate area to everything, get creative!

HIGH TRAFFIC AREAS AND NOISE CONSIDERATION

Whenever you are planning an office space, you must consider the high traffic areas and make allowances for noise. For example, is the printer in the best location? Is it accessible to those who need to use it, but not too disruptive to nearby workers? (Copiers can be noisy and attract conversations while people are waiting for their print outs.) You want to create areas that are conducive to the work being done. Keep this in mind when planning your office and where everyone (and everything) is being allocated.

One of the biggest distractions and drains on productivity is noise. Though noise is inevitable when so many people are working in a space at once, there are many ways to minimise it. Clever design decisions, like using sound absorption wall panels, are a great way to make sure that sounds cannot be heard between rooms and offices. If you have an open office plan, simple partitions and dividers can do wonders for acoustics and reduce noise levels for minimal cost.

Consider whether you could redesign your office to allocate specific tasks or departments to their own rooms. Some tasks or jobs may require more discussion than others. These workers should be allocated to their own area, so that those who need a quiet environment to stay focused can work in peace.

GET DRAWING!

Everything you need for a functional layout can be mapped out on paper. Have fun with this! Play with some of your own ideas before speaking with designers or a fitout company. I have included some basic thought starters below to get you going.

Many fitout companies offer layout planning in house (including us and free of charge). Take your time with the planning stage or call your fitout company and share your ideas.

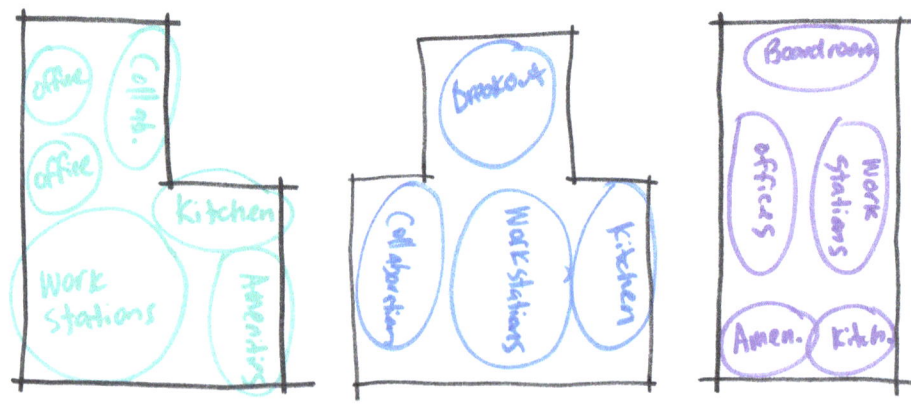

SPACE PLANNING   51

1 **Grab some grid paper.**
Draw the outline of your office. The shape will determine what can and cannot be done in the space. This does not need to be to perfect scale. Just use it as a guide.

2 **Mark out fixed items.**
Mark all entrances, exits, windows, columns, and existing bathrooms. Draw anything that cannot be moved.

3 **Decide on the big things.**
This is where you map the layout of offices, storage, utilities, printers, and the kitchen.

4 **Consider alternative layouts.**
Allow yourself to think outside the box and play with the layout.

5 **Add the finishing touches.**
Add in the final things like workstations, filing cabinets, furniture, waiting chairs, and shelving units. Is there anything you have missed?

When you are ready, head to the interactive book so you can start planning your space!

Planning for the Future

Are you planning to grow your business, or do you want to stay small?

A new office fitout is always a large investment, so you want to make sure it will stand the test of time. It is important to factor in the future needs of your business and make sure your fitout can easily adapt and grow to suit those changes. If you don't look to the future, chances are you will need fitout services again sooner rather than later.

GROWING NUMBER OF STAFF

One of the most common reasons businesses seek a new fitout is because they are hiring more employees. The layout might need to be changed to accommodate new desks and staff. Sometimes, an entirely new space is required to make way for business growth.

Make room for this growth ahead of time. Use a layout that would suit additional people and include more office furniture than you initially need. Plan for expansion early and you **will save a lot of time and money** in the long run. Future proofing little things (like ensuring enough power and data points are installed at the time of the fitout) will mean that when it is time to hire someone new, you won't be scrambling last minute to make office changes.

Our original office design accommodated for the maximum number of staff we wanted (being a total of 12). Three years later, we hired employee number 13, 14 and 15! Thankfully, we knew a good fitout company and could quickly change the office over in a weekend. (But again, the space we initially invested in was large enough to accommodate future growth.)

TECHNOLOGY

Business must keep up with evolving technologies so that it does not get left behind. Yours is no different.

Bring your business into the 21st century by designing a fitout around the very latest technology. This may include incorporating high definition presentation equipment in the boardroom, purchasing interactive whiteboards for the offices, or making room for multiple computer screens to sit on each employee's desk.

Of course, even if you update the technology, there will always be a new and improved version not too far away. This cannot be avoided. You should still aim to implement the latest technology on the market or update it regularly, as much as your budget allows.

FLEXIBILITY

There are many ways you can make your office more flexible and adaptable to suit different working styles and changes in the workplace.

Perhaps when you started out, two departments were equal in size. However, over time, one has grown far larger than the other. In cases like this, moveable walls and partitions are ideal to segment departments easily when business priorities change.

Adjustable furniture is another 'must have' that can help promote interaction and break down private office barriers. It can also be great for health and wellness. A number of our clients have invested in sit and stand desks to give team members flexibility in how they work throughout the day.

You will also need to keep staff who work remotely in mind. Ensure that they are connected to office systems and have the ability to work from anywhere, now and into the future.

STYLE

Trends in interior design tend to change drastically over time. If you want to make sure your office will stay stylish for decades to come, stick with a simple base for your interior. You can then change up artwork and textiles to ensure your office remains current.

By sticking with neutral colours on the walls and floor, you will save time, money, and effort by only having to update decorative elements as the years roll on.

Furniture Considerations

Furniture is an (obvious) necessity. After all, what is an office without a place to actually sit or stand and work?

EXISTING, LEASED, SECOND HAND OR FURNISHED?

Some clients request to re-use existing furniture in a new fitout. This can be a smart and cost effective option. However, you should still **include a furniture allowance in your budget**, even if you don't *think* you will need it.

Many of our clients who have chosen to re-use furniture have later realised that:

1. **The fitout does not suit the layout of existing furniture and is counterproductive to team productivity.**

2. **The existing furniture suddenly looks old, dated and out of place in the new space.**

These clients have then had to come up with money *on top of* the original budget to allow for new furniture.

If you have existing office furniture that you want to discard, try selling it privately. Alternatively, you can jump on websites like Green Furniture Hub[1] or Business Recycling[2] to arrange charity collection.

Tell the fitout company that furniture removal is to be **excluded from the quote**. This will save you a lot of money. Unfortunately, second hand furniture isn't worth much in the commercial fitout industry, and it will generally cost more to remove it than to give it away.

If you are on a tight budget and can't afford to purchase new furniture right away, you might want to consider leasing furniture. If you go down this route, keep in mind that though the upfront cost may be less, it will be more expensive in the long run.

TIP

Ask your fitout company to give you separate quote for furniture that has been broken down into line item pricing. That way, if furniture has not been factored into your budget, you will at least have a list of items that you can purchase separately at a later date or worked through as construction commences on site.

You can also search second hand shops for furniture supplies. You might strike gold and find a funky preloved gem that will add to the culture of the office. Or, you could find an item that can be upcycled and function well in the workspace. This will also add character and flair to an otherwise boring space.

If you find an edgy piece that is a little worse for wear, refurbish it yourself! This could be anything from a large desk that can be converted into a boardroom table, office chairs that can be fitted with new upholstery, or a retro wooden coffee table that can be varnished and polished to look like new. Let your imagination run wild. There are hidden treasures everywhere, all you have to do is look!

You could also consider filling the office with unique pieces from your team's travel adventures to create that 'at home' feel.

Some spaces may have the option to come furnished. If this is a possibility, you can negotiate with the leasing agent as to whether the previous tenant would be open to leaving some (or all) of their furniture. Paying a little extra in rent each month is likely to work out being cheaper and easier than refurbishing the space. It is also a win for the existing tenant, as they don't need to pay someone to remove their furniture for them.

TIP

Try trawling websites like Gumtree and Facebook Marketplace for second hand items. You might be able to grab a great bargain on office desks, chairs, shelving, filing cabinets and office decor simply because it has been used before.

SIMPLE WORKSTATION POD LAYOUTS

Whether you are looking to maximise space, or want to create a more meaningful workspace, we have come up with a few furniture layouts to help make designing your office a little easier.

When choosing the most appropriate layout, you will first need to first consider:

- The size of the room

- The number of employees you have (and expect to gain in the future)

- The type of work your employees do

- The amount of privacy your employees need

- Whether (and where) you will install mobile drawer units, shelving, lighting, privacy screens, and/or modesty panels

(You may also want to flick back to Part One for further information on how your layout can impact the culture of your office.)

1. Rectangle desks

Rectangle furniture pods come in a wide variety of sizes and styles and can be completely customised. You can arrange desks in any way you like, from one large, shared rectangle desk with dividing screens, to individual tables sitting side by side, back to back, or in neat lines. This is a simple and versatile shape to work with and will suit large open areas.

One of our IT clients opted for a simple rectangle desk layout. As their work was electronic and they did not have much physical paperwork, they did not need a large amount of desk space. They saved money and space by dividing large tables into smaller work areas with partitions, allowing the one desk to be used by four people.

Some workplaces, however, will require more privacy. By installing individual dividers (or privacy screens) on the backs and sides of each work station, employees will feel less exposed. Partitions can be customised with patterns, colours, and material, and can also double as a pin board so that staff can display important reminders (or that cute puppy picture). This simple addition makes extra use of the space and reduces desk clutter.

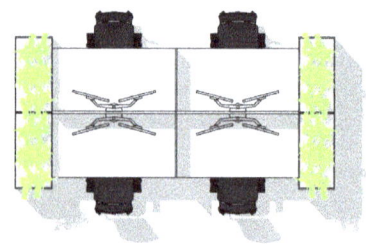

Large table with screens mounted

FURNITURE CONSIDERATIONS   57

2. Right angle workstation pods

L shaped pods provide additional desk space and improved privacy. Rather than employees sitting opposite one another (as they would at a rectangular table), colleagues work on individual desks. This means that they are not within each other's line of sight while looking at the computer screen.

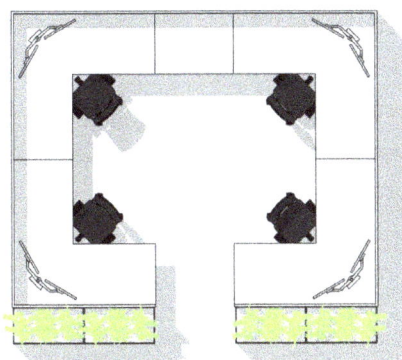

Right angle workstation pod with no dividing screens with surrounding screens

Having no partitions attached to desks can make an office space look bigger and more open. Large L shaped desks with no dividers give employees the ability to easily see and speak with fellow colleagues, and also provide them with enough space to work in.

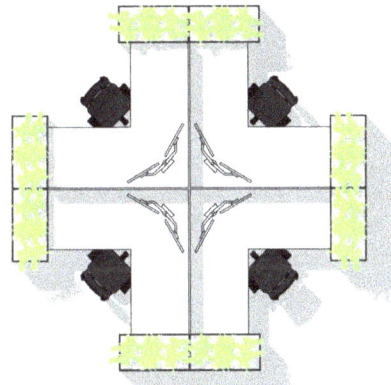

Right angle workstation pod with dividing screens

Larger work cubicle spaces can be created with four L shaped desks placed together to form a cubed office nook. When combined with high partitions, this formation can almost look like its own little office. This option is great for staff who work in teams, as it promotes collaboration but provides privacy from the rest of the office. L shaped desks can take up a large amount of room, so ensure your space is big enough if opting for this design.

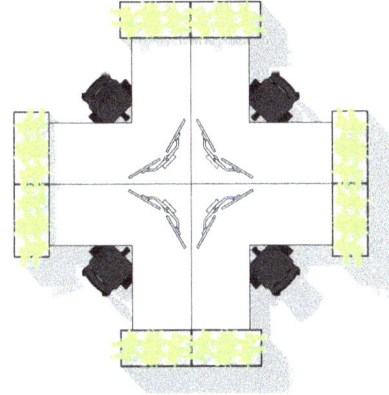

Right angle workstation pod with <u>no</u> dividing screens

3. L shaped (enclosed) workstation pod

This layout can be great for close knit teams, as the pod creates a 'unit' feeling. However, some employees may feel claustrophobic in this arrangement, as there is only one entry and exit point. Further, this design can leave team members feeling isolated, as communication with the wider office may be adversely affected.

This design would work well if people were coming together to work on a combined project, but did not need to be secluded from the rest of the office for an extended period.

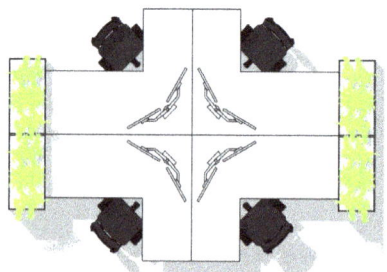

L-shaped workstation pod with no dividing screens

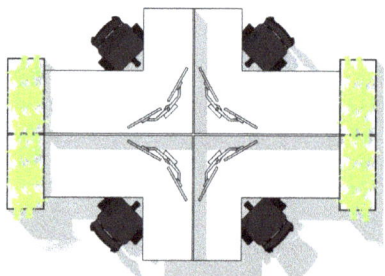

L-shaped workstation pod with dividing screens

4. 120 Degree Workstations

These desks are popular for odd shaped buildings. They are highly practical can be extended easily to create another pod of three.

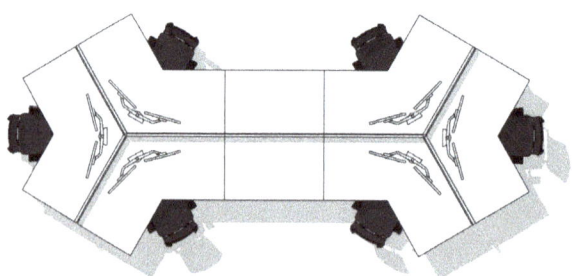

120° Workstation pod

5. **Curved pods**

   This layout is similar to the enclosed L shaped pod, except there is more room for team members. A unique (and rare) design, a curved pod will make your office space stand out (and look like a space station). Choosing a non-traditional curved desk will add flair to your office, while still delivering the same practicalities and functionalities of a standard cubicle and desk.

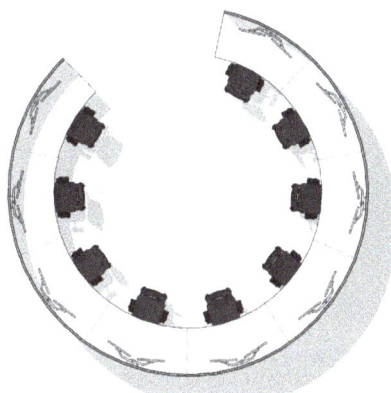

Circular workstation pod

Ergonomics and Productivity

You have now decided on the work station layout, allowed for future growth (or contraction), and determined how the flexibility of desk configuration suits the space. Now, let's explore ergonomics and why every workplace needs to consider it.

As a business owner, you might hear the term 'ergonomics' thrown around every now and then. But what exactly is it, and why is it so important for your workplace?

Ergonomics is all about improving the health, safety, productivity, and comfort of the people in your office and their interaction with technology, other employees, clients, and the environment around them. It also includes protecting staff health and welfare.

For many workplaces, ergonomic work stations are necessary to meet workplace health and safety requirements. By making your office ergonomic, staff will be less likely to experience work related injuries or health issues such as headaches, eye strains, neck pain, and back pain.

Having a work station that is comfortable to sit at can boost productivity and retention rates, and reduce absenteeism resulting from health risks (such as those listed above). When employees have a safe and comfortable space to work in, job satisfaction and morale increases, resulting in a happier and more fulfilling workplace overall.

WHAT MAKES A WORK STATION ERGONOMIC?

An ergonomic work station involves correctly setting up and positioning the office chair, monitors, desk, keyboard, mouse, and phone so that the desk is comfortable to sit at and use. This will reduce workplace repetitive strain injuries, headaches, and other related issues caused by poor posture and discomfort. It may also extend to providing items like foot rests, mouse and keyboard wrist support pads, screen dimmers, and headsets so that commonly used items can be accessed with ease and comfort.

As you read this, you might be fretting over the expense of buying these items for every employee. There is no denying that making your office ergonomic comes at a cost. However, when you genuinely care for your staff and go out of your way to look after their needs, the result is increased productivity, staff happiness, and better performance.

Many office furniture options can be specifically designed to meet ergonomic standards. Ideal office furniture is adjustable and can be easily modified to accommodate different needs and job requirements. What type of setup suits you best will depend on the work tasks being performed, the design and adjustability of the equipment, and your existing office layout. For example, a factory worker will require a different set up to an office worker.

IS MY WORK STATION ERGONOMICALLY CORRECT?

Try making these adjustments while sitting at your desk!

MONITOR
When sitting at your office desk, the monitor should be roughly an arm's length away. The top of the monitor should be at, or just below, eye level.

DESK
There should be plenty of leg room and knee space under your desk so that you can change positions easily. The surface of the desk should be big enough to hold all necessary day-to-day items including your computer, phone, stationery, and paperwork. Cables should be neatly tied and secured.

KEYBOARD
When using the keyboard, your elbows should be close to your body. There should be minimal bend in your wrists, and the elbows should be angled between 90 and 120 degrees. Wrist and/or mouse pads may be useful for some staff.

CHAIR
The ideal seat is an adjustable swivel chair with five feet and castor wheels. When sitting in the chair, the back should be straight. The backrest should support the lower back comfortably.

LEGS AND FEET

Feet should either be flat on the ground or resting on a footrest. Make sure that the front of the chair does not press on the back of the knees.

For more on how to set up an ergonomic work station, take a look at these guidelines included in the Interactive Book and carry out an assessment on your team and workspace.

WHY INVEST IN SIT STAND DESKS?

Sit stand desks are a great alternative to stationary desks, as they give employees the flexibility to choose how they work throughout the day. Staff can stretch their legs without taking a break or interrupting workflow. Sit stand desks (when used correctly) can help combat fatigue, increase productivity, relieve muscle tension, and improve posture.

There are two main types of sit stand desks: manual and electronic. As the name suggests, manual sit stand desk are moved up and down by hand, usually by a lever. The employee winds the lever to adjust the height of the desk. This can become heavy and tiresome, which may deter use.

Electronic desks, on the other hand, can be raised and lowered with the touch of a button. These days, many models come with a pre-set feature, which enables the employee to save their standing and seated heights.

If you are not sure whether you should invest in a sit stand desk (maybe you purchased new desks not that long ago) you might consider installing portable platforms on top of your existing desks. These platforms will still give employees the option to sit or stand during the day, but will be cheaper and lighter than an entire sit stand desk.

Keep in mind that because these platforms are smaller, they won't be suitable for employees who have a lot of physical paperwork. These desks will suit staff who use limited equipment and work on a single screen or laptop during the day.

TIP

Consider spending a little extra on ergonomic chairs as they will support your employees' posture and allow them to feel comfortable throughout the day. Poorly designed office chairs do more harm than good, and could end up costing you more in the long run due to your staff having to take time off work to get better and realigned. Choose chairs that are adjustable, comfortable, and support the spine.

Planning for Light and Airflow

Natural light is a priceless commodity in the office. However, not everyone has the luxury of it pouring into the workspace through windows. In fact, some offices have no windows at all.

For offices that have very little, or no, natural light, there are a few things you can do to make sure your staff still receive the benefits that a brightly lit space would offer. Play around with some of these ideas if your office is lacking natural light and see the magnificent difference just a small change can make.

Having the right bulbs in the right places can create the illusion of natural light. If you are using cubicle separators, illuminate each individual workspace with an ambient glow that is not harsh on the eyes.

If your office is open plan, using overhead lights is a must. Add extra light to places where more shadows are cast. You want to make sure that there is an even distribution of light across an open plan floor.

Another clever way to incorporate natural light is to use white, bright, and light colours on the walls. White painted walls are usually the most common choice. Add splashes of colour with artwork or fabric to take the boring out and create the illusion of more light. Place spotlights over plants or certain areas for emphasis.

Glass partitioning will keep your space feeling modern and will allow natural light to flow through the office where it can. Mirrors and internal glass can also give an illusion of brightness by reflecting the light from inside the office. This naturally makes the space look a lot bigger than it is.

Of course, it is much more beneficial to find a space with natural light. Natural light has proven benefits, including increased productivity, health, and wellbeing in the workplace. Everybody needs an adequate amount of daylight per day. It is crucial for the body's

TIP

Consider scheduling walking meetings so that everyone can benefit from fresh air and natural light!

circadian rhythm and improves mood, reduces stress, and increases intake of vitamin D.

If your office is quite dark and lacking in natural light, encourage employees to step outside during breaks to take a stretch and a walk. The space where your employees spend the most time should be the best lit room in the office.

It is important to have the right lighting to ensure that your staff do not experience eye fatigue or headaches. Make sure lighting is appropriate for the space and that the office is well lit and conducive to the work. You can also adapt lighting to the type of mood you are trying to encourage. In certain spaces (like a meditation room) you may prefer dim lighting, whereas in a working space, natural light is much more beneficial to creating a nurturing environment.

It is important to create a balanced atmosphere that is not too relaxed or too busy. Decide how you want the office to feel and go with it.

KEEP IT MODERN

When you undertake a fitout, you do it to last (at least seven to ten years) so you want it to stay looking fresh and modern. Keep your new fitout looking up to date by using a timeless, basic layout with a simple colour scheme. You can always update fixtures, fittings, furniture, and small items easily and on a budget.

Most commercial products will keep fitouts looking modern as they can be easily replaced if damaged, dated, or in need of refreshing. For example, ceiling tiles that have been water damaged can be replaced individually in a single section, without the need to redo the entire ceiling. The same goes for carpet tiles or vinyl planks. Worn or stained areas can simply be replaced with a few new tiles, so you won't need to order an expensive roll of broadloom carpet to cover the entire area.

Glazing films and wallpapers are another simple and cost effective solution to keep your space looking modern. Use these materials to add patterns and colours to the walls in your office and create illusions, corporate branding, or frosted privacy screens.

You could also try and create different moods in specific areas of the office. For example, a mural displaying a wall of trees with the sun coming through the leaves may evoke feelings of peace, calm and tranquillity, as well as give an illusion of natural light. A peaceful **beach and water scene may give off a** sense of calm and new energy.

There are some great wallpaper products available that are simple to apply, and even easier to peel off and replace. These are great if you have different marketing messages or service delivery and want to have the flexibility to change what is displayed. Think of retailers who use similar signs in their windows to market sales each season. Other facilities, like hospitals, use replaceable wallpaper to display the logos of their key donors. These backgrounds are interchangeable and quick to replace when new photos with sponsors are needed.

KEEP IT SIMPLE!

You don't want an empty office, but you definitely *do not* want a cluttered one either. Think about how you can strike a balance between the two by using a simple design that allows everyone to be able to express themselves without feeling cramped. (Design and decorating will be discussed in detail later in this book!)

Have fun and let your imagination run wild!

> **TIP**
>
> ☆ Installing carpet and vinyl tiles in particularly high traffic areas is a great option. It is easy to replace a single section following wear and tear!
>
> ☆ Ask your fitout company to leave any left-over carpet tiles or request that a box of carpet and ceiling tiles are provided to you at handover so you have replacements on hand.

FIRST IMPRESSIONS

Your brand is reflected in the quality of the finishes and furniture you choose for your office. First impressions last, and your brand needs to grab potential clients and employees as soon as they walk through the door.

The fitout will be the first thing anyone sees when entering your office. Make it count. After all, you are setting the business up for the future. Is the boardroom presentable? Are there fresh flowers at reception? What impact does the space have on visitors when they walk in?

Someone once told us, "if you want to be a world class company, everything you do must be world class." This extends to every aspect of your business, from kitchenware (those $2 Kmart tumblers just don't feel the same as heavy crystal glasses in a client meeting), to uniforms, company cars, and the way your team presents themselves.

Make the first impression of your company something that wows everyone who sees it!

ENGAGING A FITOUT COMPANY CHECKLIST

You have planned everything and have decided to make the investment and proceed with a fitout. How exciting! Now, before you go and sign the first fitout company you find, read this section to make sure that you are asking all the right questions.

I am sure you have heard the horror stories about contractors. Costly overruns, time delays, hidden fees, poor quality – the list goes on. But it doesn't have to be this way! Give yourself the best chance of having a positive fitout experience by engaging the right company from the beginning. After all, installing a new fitout should be an exciting time, not a stressful one.

Compare at least two or three quotes before engaging a fitout company. However, keep in mind that the cheapest price does not always reflect best value for money. Cost should never be the only factor considered when choosing which fitout company to go with.

TEN THINGS TO CONSIDER PRIOR TO ENGAGING A FITOUT COMPANY

1. Capability, experience and previous projects

With many elements needing to come together to pull off an outstanding fitout, it takes a developed and unique skill set to manage such a project.

Proper planning and design are important parts of any fitout. The company you choose must be well established in their processes and have enough experience so that they are well equipped to handle any size or type of fitout. Many fitout companies specialise in certain sectors, so it is important that you know which fitout company will be right for you. For example, a retail, hospitality or medical fitout will require a very different skillset to an office one.

It is always best to see what other fitouts the company has completed in similar spaces or industries. That way, you can get an idea of the quality of work they can produce for you. (You might even get some ideas on how you can improve your own space.)

2. Services

Does the fitout company offer an all-in-one service? A good fitout company will be able to handle everything including design, project management, construction, coordination of tradespeople, and resource scheduling to ensure that your project is finished on time and to the highest quality. They should be able to handle refurbishments, 'make-goods', and de-fits across a range of sectors.

The fitout company should also offer additional services, like supplying and installing office furniture, shelving, and storage. They might even place some artwork and plants around the office to make it look a bit more special. Essentially, you want to engage a fitout company that will be able to handle everything for you so that you have the confidence to take a hands off approach. They may even offer valuable insights and ideas that you never considered before.

> Consider and plan everything in detail and ensure it is all to a world class standard.

3. **Team resources and capacity**

    Good fitout companies are often very busy! It is important that you understand their resources, workloads, and team capacity to ensure that the required amount of time and personnel can be dedicated to your fitout.

    Ask to meet the project delivery team and request a list of their current project workloads and time committed to each. A reputable company will have enough resources to dedicate to your project (and should be able to provide a 'backup staff' of the key project team members). It is also worthwhile to request corporate resumes of the project delivery team members to better understand their experience, particularly if your project is complex.

    Will you be assigned a **dedicated project manager** to look after your fitout from start to finish, or will they be busy running around on other jobs? A committed project manager will be 100% focused on completing your fitout on time, on budget, and to the highest standard. Ensure that your fitout company provides this.

4. **Reviews, testimonials and transparency**

    When it comes to choosing a business or service of any kind, you can't beat word of mouth referrals and genuine reviews from clients. Ask other businesses that have completed fitouts for their recommendations, and search for reviews and testimonials on fitout company websites. You can also look at Google reviews and reviews listed on social media accounts. Feel free to ask previous clients to contact you for an honest review.

    Any quality fitout business should be completely transparent about the service they provide and what it is that they do. Your first impression of the business will likely be through their website. If they have plenty of information about the service they provide and what you can expect when working with them, that is a good start. When you have your first chat with the company (either over the phone or in person), they should be able to answer all of your questions openly and honestly.

5. Understanding your requirements

When reviewing the proposal or quote provided by your preferred fitout company, make sure that a **detailed scope of work** has been included. Read through this thoroughly and check whether you (or the fitout company) have made any assumptions. For example, you may have assumed that the offices will be partitioned with glass, however the fitout company has only allowed for plasterboard (as it is a cheaper option).

Some companies will provide you with a concept design as well as a detailed scope of works. This is one of the best ways to be clear on expectations and what has been covered in the quote. These documents will ensure that all parties are clear on the project's requirements from the outset, and that the costs reflect the drawings. A thorough concept design and scope of works may also avoid variations down the track.

Another common misunderstanding are assumptions about **work after hours**. As a business owner, it might sound ideal to have all work carried out after the office has shut for the day or on weekends. However, this does come at a higher cost. A good fitout company will be used to working in occupied spaces with minimal disruption to staff. If you require after hours work, ensure that this is communicated upfront and make sure the fitout company is equipped to handle this request.

Stay on budget. The last thing you want is to receive unexpected variations, especially if these items were originally discussed but never made it into the scope of work. Choose a fitout company that keeps your best interests front of mind. They should work with you during the fee proposal and design phase, and provide you with a clear and precise scope of the work to be done. You will know that you are working with a good company if they provide design alternatives, suggest ways to save on cost, give buildability advice, suggest small design changes, and stick to your budget throughout the process.

6. Insurances, licences and awards

At a minimum, the company you are looking to engage must hold **relevant licences** (the requirements are different in each state).

It is important to check the licence category and confirm the fitout company are actually qualified to carry out the works. In addition, check their licence history for any suspensions, exclusions, directions to rectify defective work, disciplinary actions, or infringement notices.

Secondly, **insurances** are essential. Ensure you request a copy of all certificates of currency and check their expiry dates, whether they are current, and if they have any limitations. Not only is insurance a mandatory requirement for contractors, it will also protect you if something doesn't go to plan.

Having a high status and strong reputation in the industry speaks volumes about the fitout business you are dealing with. It is a big tick if they have won any **key business or industry awards**. The application process for a business award is gruelling. It takes a well organised and executed company to even gather the information required to submit an application. Businesses are then scrutinised by judges (made up of some of the industry's top representatives) and put up against other businesses in their category. An award-winning company speaks for itself.

A little brag...

Future Fitouts was named a finalist in the **Telstra Business Awards (#TelstraBizAwards), Telstra Women's Awards, Lord Mayor of Brisbane Business Awards, was a Westpac Top 200 Winner** and has been recognised in many other business and industry awards!

7. **Certifications (including Workplace Health and Safety)**

It is worth finding out if the fitout company is ISO (International Organization for Standardization) certified and whether they have management systems and certificates of proof to support this. The most common certifications in this industry are:

- Workplace, Health & Safety Management System
- Quality Management System
- Environment Management System

An ISO certification instantly adds credibility to a business as it shows that a product or service meets client expectations. You may not find too many fitout companies that have this, as maintaining this level of certification takes time, commitment, annual audits, and a lot of system upkeep.

If the company is not certified, at minimum request a copy of their Site Specific Safety Management Plan to understand their commitment to safety and your project.

8. Systems and reporting

Understanding what types of systems and reporting functions are in place will assist you in your decision making. Is there someone higher than the project manager that you would be able to raise concerns with? What systems does the company use to manage quality, consistency, and timeframes?

Ongoing communication is vital. You should always be kept informed on how the fitout is progressing from start to finish. Ensure that you will receive regular reporting updates and invitations to on site meetings so that you can keep up to date with your project.

The process should be smooth and easy for you (that is why you are engaging the experts in the first place). Having peace of mind that they are a systemised and organised company will assist with this.

9. Timely delivery

Fitout companies are generally used to working to tight deadlines. Ensure that the company you work with has the resources to commit to and deliver your new space in a timely manner in accordance with your deadlines. If you have a set date (whether this be a move in date, opening date, launch party date, or key date associated with your lease) it is crucial the fitout company is aware so that they meet these commitments. Request a detailed project gantt chart (also known as a construction program) to confirm the delivery.

10. Professional and reliable

The final consideration comes down to the interactions and dealings you have had with the fitout company. Do you feel like you will be working with a professional, reputable, and reliable company?

Right attitude: Is the fitout team approachable? Do they listen to your specific needs and deliver to your brief? It is important that the fitout you receive matches what you want to achieve in your space. After all, it is your business, and you should have a say in how your fitout looks.

Trust and integrity: Do you have a positive gut feeling when you meet with the company? Do you hold a level of trust in their services? First impressions count. If the fitout company is transparent and upfront about their service from the very beginning, you will be more inclined to trust them with your fitout job.

What to Expect From the Fitout Process

BE WARNED, IT GETS UGLY!

I am not going to lie or sugar coat anything. The actual fitout process is not fun or enjoyable! Almost overnight, your space will turn into a construction site. It becomes messy and dusty. You will have trades people coming and going, additional vehicles parked at your premises, and multiple deliveries per day. If you are still occupying and working from the space (which is very common) you should expect some level of disruption.

Most fitout companies will be accustomed to working in occupied spaces and will put methods in place to work effectively while protecting you and other tenants in the building (such as arranging for certain noisy works to occur after hours). I recommend you have conversations around the expected disruptions, any car parks that are restricted (the last thing you want is a ute parked in the boss's spot), and whether there are specific rules you or the contractors should follow. That way, everyone will be on the same page and any disruptions can be managed appropriately.

HAVE YOU MADE THE RIGHT DECISION?

Questions to answer	NO	YES
Does the company have proven experience completing similar sized fitouts?	❏	❏
Have you seen evidence of successful fitouts for similar businesses (on their website, capability statement, or social pages)?	❏	❏
Have they performed fitouts for your industry before?	❏	❏
Are reputable clients and previously completed works displayed on the fitout company's website?	❏	❏
Have they worked with any well-known clients or reputable brands?	❏	❏
Do they offer a full and comprehensive list of services (including design, project management, coordination, construction, and handover)?	❏	❏
Have you met the project delivery team?	❏	❏
Are you comfortable with the resource strategy and the team's experience?	❏	❏
Will you be assigned a dedicated project manager who is your one point of contact and is available throughout the project?	❏	❏
Have you been provided with a 'backup' delivery team?	❏	❏
Have you checked the company's reviews and/or spoken to previous clients for a referral?	❏	❏

Does the fitout company have a plan to manage works and minimise disruptions during normal business hours so that you can remain in operation?	❏	❏
Have you received (and reviewed) a detailed scope of work that is clear and meets all of your requirements?	❏	❏
Does the fitout company have certifications for Workplace Health and Safety, Quality, and Environment Management Systems?	❏	❏
Does the fitout company have the resources to meet your project deadlines?	❏	❏
Do you have a good gut feeling and a professional first impression?	❏	❏

Total _____

Add up the total number of yeses. Use the key below to work out whether your fitout company is right for you.

More than 12: Great job! You are in good hands and have found a fantastic company to work with! Your fitout should be an exciting and (relatively) stress free experience.

Between nine and 12: It's not a deal breaker, but your fitout company could be better. Is there anything you can ask or negotiate with your fitout company to make sure that they provide you with a premium service? Can they give you any additional sureties or guarantees? If not, it might be wise to keep looking around.

Less than eight: Steer clear of this fitout company! Keep looking – you will eventually find the right one!

MY OWN WORST CLIENT

It is our business to understand client requirements and transform spaces. However, we are also fortunate enough to have been on the 'client side' of things. It is safe to say that I have a new appreciation of what our client's go through!

It was such an exciting time. We had just picked up the keys to our dream office and had all of these amazing ideas of what we could do with it. We wanted to create a 'Google inspired' office fitout!

I was concerned about budget and the cost of making too many changes to the existing layout. I was worried about managing the process, getting the design right, future proofing for staff growth, choosing the right colour scheme, and everything in between (basically, everything our clients go through on every fitout).

I said to Aaron, "let's just keep the existing fitout. It's usable. We can make it work."

Before

He got sick of telling me that our business is this industry. We do fitouts every day, so we needed an office that showcased what we could do with a space.

We went back and forth over the design. Eventually, we came to an agreement and works commenced on site. Now, in the fitout game, things happen quickly and sometimes all at once!

I remember arriving two or three days later to see the progress. I couldn't believe the mess! Aaron's famous words, "trust me, it will look worse before it looks better" could not have been more true.

What was a presentable office a few days prior was now a dusty and unpleasant construction zone. Cables were hanging from the roof, walls had been completely knocked out, air conditioning ducts lined the floor, rubbish was thrown across the room, and the car park was filled with utes. Somehow, the nice marble bathrooms (that weren't even part of the scope) were also full of dirt and dust!

I don't know why I was so shocked. I have been in the construction industry for many years and have spent lots of time on site (including for our own fitout jobs). But this was different. I wasn't the builder or project manager in this scenario. I was the client.

A few days later, I visited the site again. The joiners were finalising the kitchen cabinets and I realised that we hadn't allowed room for an oven. I asked them to stop work.

Now, it's not common to have an oven in an office fitout (hence why it wasn't shown on the design). I convinced Aaron that we needed one to heat up food on Friday afternoons for team functions (a decision he will now admit was a good one). However, asking the joiners to stop midway through and change the layout was considered variation and caused a time delay.

There were many disagreements between Aaron and I during our own fitout. It was a stressful process and I was one of our worst clients. But, eventually, it all came together and now we LOVE it. The improvement our office fitout made to staff morale, culture, turnover, and performance was incredible. We created a space filled with bright colours that people enjoy being in! The space is modern, roomy, and includes areas for team exercise, celebration, and fun. We used an open plan layout to encourage collaboration and teamwork.

I have lost count of the number of visitors, sales representatives, clients, and delivery drivers who walk into our office and say, "wow, this is a cool space," or, "it's so nice to be in an office that is fun and vibrant!" The most common question we get is "are you guys hiring?"

Lessons I learnt from our own fitout:

1. Agree on the design and details before construction starts. (It will cost you time and money if you make changes later.)

2. Expect disruption, mess, noise, and short-term pain. (The finished product after the final clean will all be worth it!)

3. Most importantly – leave it to the fitout professionals! (It's not worth the stress and headache to try and manage it yourself.)

After

Office De-Fit and Make Goods Checklist (Only applicable if leasing)

When moving offices, it is likely that you will experience an office de-fit or 'make good' (as it is commonly known in the industry).

As long as you are organised and plan ahead, you will not have to worry about it going astray. To keep you on track, we have compiled a list of things you should consider throughout the make good process.

ALWAYS REFER TO YOUR LEASE AGREEMENT

If you are ever in doubt or unsure about how much you are required to do for your de-fit, refer to your agreement. The make good requirements should be clearly stipulated in the lease with your landlord. Usually, the standard agreement is that the premises must be restored to its original condition (i.e. the condition at the time you commenced occupation), or back to its 'base shell'. Original condition can include restoring the colour of the walls, the floor coverings and removing any modifications you have made to the space. Basically, you should return the space back as a blank canvas, just as you acquired it. If you are still in doubt, contact your estate agent or landlord to make sure you are covered. Make sure all communications are in writing.

TIP

If you have built a fitout that may be attractive to the next tenant, try to negotiate your way out of the make good clause and agree on a cash settlement with your landlord. A cash settlement is always the cheaper and more efficient option.

DON'T BECOME COMPLACENT ABOUT THE MAKE GOOD OBLIGATIONS

Many business owners will get so excited about their new premises, that they neglect the one they are in and forget about the make good requirements. To ensure you are on top of it, be strategic and start making arrangements as soon as possible. Get some help and delegate jobs to others. Put a little bit of money away for this.

KEEP TRACK OF ALL CHANGES

As soon as you move into the new premises, take note of all the changes you make. This can be done any way you like. I find that referring to the fitout plans is an easy way to keep track of any alterations. Then, when it is time for you to move out and make good, you will know exactly what needs to go and what stays. It is always good practice to keep before and after photographs, especially if you already know the space is temporary (a bit like a residential entry condition report).

Even if you think that you will occupy the space long term, you should still get into the habit of keeping a log of all your changes. You may need to move out because the space is too small for your growing business, or you might find a better location to relocate to. There are many reasons you may want a change in the future. So, to be safe and keep on top of things, it is a great idea to have all the information you need on hand.

HAVE A MAKE GOOD LIST

Keeping records, photos, plans, and a list of all the things to do for the de-fit process is a great way to make sure that nothing gets missed. Some of the most common things that may need to be changed, removed, or repainted include:

- Bulkheads
- Joinery
- Walls and doors
- Partitions
- Windows
- Frosting and decals
- Floor coverings
- Fittings and fixtures
- Ceilings
- Layout

Once you have completed all repairs and restorations, you will then need to complete a thorough final clean of the premises.

As soon as you think that the de-fit has been completed, make sure that the building manager or landlord signs off on the completion and satisfaction of the make good requirements.

ASK A PROFESSIONAL
You may like to undertake the whole de-fit process on your own. However, it really does pay off in the long run to hire a professional to help you out.

When you do things on your own, you risk doing more damage, especially when it comes to removing fixtures and fittings. If that happens, fixing the mistake could end up costing more. Take the time to research some professionals and do not be afraid to ask for help.

Hiring a second pair of hands may just keep your sanity so that you can focus on doing what you love (running your business).

Preparing for a Fitout and Moving Tips

No one likes moving!

MONTHS BEFORE THE FITOUT OR MOVE
So, you have signed a new lease or purchased a new space. Congratulations! Now it is time to start planning your move (and the fitout). Make the moving process as smooth and pain free as possible by getting these necessary tasks out of the way well in advance.

KEEP STAFF INFORMED.
Start by organising a team who are coordinating the move and schedule a meeting to get everyone on board. It is important that the entire staff know what is going on, so that they are prepared by the time moving day rolls around.

LET CLIENTS AND RELEVANT SERVICES KNOW ABOUT YOUR MOVE.
Inform your clients, investors, vendors, delivery services, utilities, and affiliates of your intention to move and confirm the new address and moving date with them.

PUT A MOVE KIT TOGETHER

This moving kit should include:

- A floor plan marked with the names of rooms and team members' desks. These names are then written on boxes, furniture, and equipment so that things can be easily placed in the new premises.

- A contact list for all people and contractors involved in the move.

- A program of when things need to happen (especially if it is a large project with staged moves).

- A plan for IT. Consider shut down, relocation, and turn on at the new space. When is the downtime and do all staff know about it?

- A furniture and equipment register, so that everything is accounted for.

- Moving essentials including packing boxes, wrapping tape, bubble wrap, newspaper, labels, and permanent markers.

BOOK A REMOVALIST

Removalists are invaluable as they can pack (if needed), have flexible hours, and are experts at moving. Rather than trying to move yourself, it really pays to have professionals help you with the moving process. Make sure you get a rundown on the relocation protocol from the removalist company and discuss any specific preparations with them beforehand so that the move is as smooth as possible on the day.

TIMING YOUR MOVE

Make sure moving day is not aligned with an important event or key company milestone that could be disruptive to the moving process. Try timing your move during a slow period for your business, so there is as little disruption as possible.

Remember to cancel subscriptions and update your billing and delivery address with all service providers. (This may include cleaners, toilet sanitary services, gardeners, and regular service repairs.)

MINIMISE DOWN TIME

Try to coordinate as much out of hours relocation as possible to minimise disruptions and downtime for your business.

SPEAK WITH YOUR FITOUT PROJECT MANAGER

Consider completing the office fitout before your staff move into the new space. If this isn't possible, you may need to arrange for the fitout to be completed outside of work hours.

Spend some time liaising with your fitout project manager to determine the ideal space planning for your new office. To do this, consider the departments or teams that need to sit in close proximity to each other. Get some input from your employees to make sure that they will be happy with the new layout.

WEEKS AND DAYS BEFORE THE MOVE

CLEAN AND DECLUTTER YOUR OFFICE

Spring clean the office and scale down on unwanted items. Start with common areas first, and leave day-to-day office essentials until last.

The big clean out should be a team effort. Staff members should empty their desks, drawers, cupboards, fridge, and pantry. Items that are being kept (but don't need to be accessed before moving day) should be set aside or placed into moving boxes.

KEYS

New keys and key cards should be distributed to staff members who will be opening and locking up the new premises.

I.T AND PHONES

Arrange to have your IT and phone lines transferred to the new premises so that everything is set up and ready to go by the time your staff are settled into the new office. Fitout companies rarely get involved with the IT and phone side of the business, so ensure they are involved in the process so everyone is up and running in a short space of time.

ON MOVING DAY

ACCOUNT FOR UNEXPECTED DELAYS

Make sure you allow extra time for the move, as delays often arise.

REMOVALIST INSTRUCTIONS

Make sure your removalist has clear instructions on where things should be placed in your new space.

Someone from your office should always be contactable on moving day. That way, the removalist will have access to someone who can help answer any questions or concerns as soon as possible.

CHANGE OF ADDRESS
Change your address details on your website, social media channels, business cards, and promotional materials.

AFTER THE MOVE
Once everything has been fully relocated to your new destination, you will need to start the process of stripping out your old premises. Make good any changes that you have made to your previous space before handing back the keys to ensure you get your security bond back.

Avoiding Additional Costs

MISTAKES TO AVOID
Having undergone a move and office fitout ourselves, we understand that additional and unexpected costs can occur. This section is designed to help you avoid common mistakes so that there are no surprises when you get your bill at the end of the fitout process.

A fitout can be an expensive venture. It is often those costs that deter many businesses from making the leap in the first place. However, moving and refurbishing a space is often the much needed change that many businesses need to do better.

Here are some ways that you can prevent a nightmare fitout, and instead enjoy a manageable and exciting experience.

GOING IT ALONE AND NOT GETTING PROFESSIONAL HELP
Don't expect to cut costs by cutting corners. Although you may think that you are saving money by doing it all on your own, you may just end up with expensive DIY disasters or an unsatisfactory finished product. Your business deserves better than that.

A complete commercial fitout can get out of hand quickly, and every mistake that occurs during the process comes at a price. It therefore pays to have quality contractors who know what they are doing, and a professional project manager to coordinate the whole thing.

Many business owners underestimate the expertise and unique set of skills required to take on an office fitout project. The person managing the fitout needs to consider various factors and juggle many moving parts, including health and safety, subcontractors, materials, engaging stakeholders, design, and layout. It is almost always worthwhile to take advantage of the unique insights a professional fitout project manager has to offer.

Most fitout companies (including Future Fitouts) have built up long standing relationships with subcontractors. Because we provide such a high amount of work to them throughout the year, they keep their rates competitive, rather than contracting to one client as a 'one off'. We also have a bit of push and shove with them to ensure the works are delivered on time.

CHOOSE THE RIGHT BUILDING SPACE

It always helps if you can choose a space that already has a large chunk of the fitout work done for you. The less work that needs to be done, the more cost effective it will be. Look at things like the layout, flooring, doors, and any existing bathroom and kitchen facilities. Check whether the space has any base building services (like air conditioning). If these things are in good condition and they suit your vision for the perfect office, you will cut costs immediately.

POOR PLANNING

The most important piece of advice we can give you is to plan ahead. No matter how small (or large) you intend your fitout to be, it always pays to get everything in order ahead of time. This makes it much easier to manage your costs so that expenses don't get out of control.

The planning stage helps you iron out any potential issues that may pop up throughout the fitout process, and will also provide you with a budget to work with. By planning your design ahead of time, you can avoid ad hoc work that looks distasteful or is dysfunctional. If you rush through the planning stage too quickly, the fitout may end up costing you more in the end. (Keep in mind that all commercial spaces need to meet Australian standards in terms of doorway clearances, circulation and access widths.)

When planning, remember to make the landlord aware of your fitout plans to ensure you have the approval required to go ahead with your upgrades.

Speak to your preferred fitout company about their quieter periods as fees might be lowered accordingly. On the flip side, if you want your fitout finished before Christmas or the end of the financial year (the two busiest periods in the building industry), be sure to get in early. Start planning consultations with your fitout company as soon as possible so that you can lock in your project and not miss out.

NOT PRIORITISING LAYOUT AND DESIGN

The rooms and furniture that make up an office can't just be placed anywhere. Everything needs to be laid out logically so that each area is comfortable, flows, and works in a functional manner. Essentially, the overall layout should make sense and nothing should seem out of place. Determining the layout of your office should never be overlooked.

Without effective layout and design planning in place, even large spaces can seem cluttered and disorganised. Something as simple as adding glass partitioning or painting walls in cooler colours can make the space seem larger and more welcoming. To guarantee a functional and aesthetically pleasing office, we recommend working with an interior designer or architect.

BUDGET BLOWOUT

Having a comprehensive budget in place before undertaking a fitout is a must. The budget should include all costs and be advised by someone you trust. Otherwise, you might risk spending more than you need to, or not having enough cash left to finish the job.

When deciding your budget, allow some wiggle room to cover any unexpected problems or delays. Once your budget is set, don't forget to keep your finances in check. It can be very easy to get carried away and lose sight of the amount of money you have available to complete the work.

There is nothing worse than an incomplete fitout because you ran out of money. Work within your means and be realistic about what you can expect from your specified budget.

Request that the fitout company provides you with a progress claim schedule showing a breakdown of when claims are expected to be sent, and their approximate amounts. Make sure you also determine the deposit amount upfront. Unlike residential builders, commercial builders can charge any amount for a deposit on works. (This is the case in Queensland. Check the rules surrounding deposits for your relevant State of Territory.)

FAILING TO CONSULT WITH THE LANDLORD

Landlords can hinder your fitout plans if they have certain restrictions or building requirements in place. One common example is the use of incumbent or building manager preferred trades. Fitout companies are used to working with nominated subcontractors and will manage this process on your behalf and directly with the building manager.

Make sure you take the time to read over your lease agreement carefully and consult with your landlord before undergoing the fitout to avoid any barriers to the project's completion.

By making the landlord aware of your fitout plans ahead of time, you will be able to plan ahead and easily overcome any hurdles that may present themselves along the way.

NOT ENOUGH POWER AND DATA POINTS

Imagine how frustrating it would be to realise that there are not enough power or data points in the office (a *very* common oversight). This is easily preventable with appropriate planning. Running additional power and data points during the fitout stage will be a lot less costly than having them installed after the fitout has been completed.

It is always recommended to have at least two data points and double power points (or quad power) at each workstation (consider the outlets needed to power a computer, two monitors, as well as personal phones and laptops). You might also like to add power points to areas that will not be in immediate use, but can be adapted as your business grows in the future. Installing power points in common areas is another useful addition as this will enable staff to work from laptops and charge them nearby.

NOT LOOKING TO THE FUTURE

When undertaking an office fitout, many business owners fail to look to the future to see how the office space can adapt to the needs of the business.

There is nothing worse than being locked into a lease only to realise that your business has very quickly outgrown it. Leave room for expansion and plan ahead by making sure your office has space to add additional desks when more staff members come on board.

By having some foresight, you will stand out as a savvy business owner with a vision for the future.

PART THREE

GROW AND IMPROVE CULTURE

(There's positivity in the air!)

Culture

Remember in *Part One* when we briefly discussed designing your culture? This next section will delve a little deeper into looking at different ways that culture can be promoted and cultivated throughout every aspect of your business.

It really is the little things that make the difference. Culture needs to be everywhere: within the team, between employees, and in your interactions with clients. Your brand, marketing, and the space you have created all need to capture the culture that you are trying to create.

YOUR ONLINE BUSINESS PRESENCE

Marketing is important. People make assumptions about you through your social media and internet presence and clients often come to you based on your online persona. In the digital age, anyone who is applying for a job has already done their research, whether that be visiting your website, browsing your social pages, reading your Google reviews, or watching your YouTube channel. Whatever you put online is a portrayal of your business personality and paints a picture of the culture. Just like it would be very rare for an employer not to check the social pages of a potential employee, ensure that you are using social media to your advantage.

We live in an age (sometimes to our detriment) where few people have the patience to wait for their requests to be actioned (waiting longer than five minutes for an Uber can be frustrating). For businesses, it's no different. This means getting back to clients as soon as possible and ensuring that you can answer questions at any time of day (without being tied to your mobile all weekend). Do you need to be available online 24 hours a day, seven days a week? Give clients the option to message or email you any time by setting up an automated campaign or response bot to handle online queries when you are otherwise unavailable.

Marketing goes far beyond social media and there are many people who can help with online marketing strategies. If this is of interest to you, hire someone who is trained to help you obtain and retain a strong online presence. Once you have an established culture, it will be easy to generate it online and through media pages.

A Sensory Journey

Your fitout is nearly complete (or you have moved into the new premises) and it is now time to add the finishing touches. I am not talking about just slapping on some branded signage and arranging the flowers at reception (though these things are important). I want you to take it one step further. Create something special and long lasting for your team and clients by creating a unique sensory journey within your space.

I call it the 'sensory experience'. Attention to small details will ensure that your company is unique and stays in peoples' minds, even after they have left your building. It really is the little things that make a **big** difference to the work environment and motivation of your team.

Have you ever considered how your senses impact your interactions with the people around you? Or, how your mood is affected by the space that you are working in? A particular smell might make you feel happy, or the sound of an instrument could leave you feeling nostalgic. The brain creates an emotional response to the sensory triggers we experience. Our perception is based on the sensory impact of our lives. The five senses (sight, sound, smell, touch, and taste) all play a part in our learning, memory, cognitive behaviour, and physical wellbeing.

It can be very powerful to harness the senses in the right way, particularly in the workplace. In the Future Fitouts office, we have put a high emphasis on creating a sensory experience, and have seen firsthand the thriving and successful environment it manifests. Let's face it, if there is any way that we can assist our team members increase their output and productivity, we are going to do it! The best part about creating a sensory journey is that it can be done with a very minimal budget or next to no cost.

Creating a sensory experience is something anyone can do. Every office will easily be able to implement these simple ideas to make the environment more pleasant and uplifting to work in.

SIGHT
COLOUR CHOICES
A visually pleasing space is not only lovely to look at, but can also impact your mood. The aesthetics, colours, layout, and furniture pieces in your office should all come together to create a cohesive look.

Choose your colours carefully. What type of mood are you creating?

Colours are particularly important, as each can impact mood and ambience. For example, if you want to evoke a calm and productive atmosphere in the workplace, bright red and green walls are probably not going to cut it (unless, perhaps, you work in Santa's workshop at the shopping mall). Colour can influence the vibe of the office and stir up certain emotions.

Below, we have set out a list of colours and their meanings. Choose carefully to create a productive workspace.

RED

The colour of POWER

Creating excitement and a very strong first impression, red is intense, energetic, action oriented, and determined. However, red can also evoke feelings of anger and sexual passion. Use this colour strategically to get just the right balance of determination within a workplace so that it does not become too overbearing.

ORANGE

The colour of ENERGY

If you are wanting an upbeat, exciting, and enthusiastic office, then using orange is the key. Research suggests that orange increases the supply of oxygen to the brain, which can stimulate brain activity. Orange can also boost productivity and have an energising effect. This colour can also increase social communication and overall optimism. Keep in mind however, that orange can stimulate pessimism and superficiality in too large a quantity.

YELLOW

The colour of HAPPINESS

A bright colour reflecting happiness and joy, yellow can make you feel uplifted and energised. This is a great colour to use in the reception of a business as it is welcoming and evokes happiness for clients and customers. Yellow is best used sparingly, as it can create contrasting feelings of frustration, impatience and anger if there is too much of it.

GREEN

The colour of HEALTH

The colour associated with balance and growth, green induces feelings of relaxation and positivity. The negative side of green is that it can create a sense of possessiveness and wealth.

BLUE

The colour of TRUST

Calm and tranquil, blue is a stable colour associated with feelings of dependability, trust, and loyalty. This is an obvious and popular colour for many brands. Too much blue within an office space can create feelings of conservatism and opposing change, which would not be conducive within a workplace.

PURPLE

The colour of PRESTIGE

A colour that signifies royalty, prestige, and luxury. Wealth, pride, peace, and magic are also associated with the colour purple. Depending on your business, too much purple could portray the wrong message to your clients.

PINK

The colour of FUN

A very feminine colour. If you are using pink, ensure your audience is receptive to it.

GREY

The colour of MOODINESS

A very neutral and conservative colour. Grey can be associated with feelings of dullness, so should be used sparingly in an office environment. Charcoal grey can indicate masculinity.

BLACK

The colour of SOPHISTICATION

A versatile colour. Black is modern, traditional, and stable. Generally, black should be used as a base colour that can be added with other colours to create a bold and dynamic contrast. Associated with fear, power, mystery, and authority.

Research suggests that certain colours can actually improve productivity within the workplace. What colours you put in your space will depend on the type of work your employees do.

An excellent colour choice for **productivity** is **blue**. It is stable and calming and helps people focus. Choose this colour if you think it could inspire more productivity within the office.

Any **creative** industry would be wise to choose **yellow** in the office for its optimism and stimulation of creativity. Using splashes of yellow throughout the design is a great start for any creative business.

AARON'S TIP

Save your decision power in the morning. Find a shirt you love (either branded or plain) and purchase five of the exact same shirts to wear every day to the office. You won't need to think about what to wear ever again!

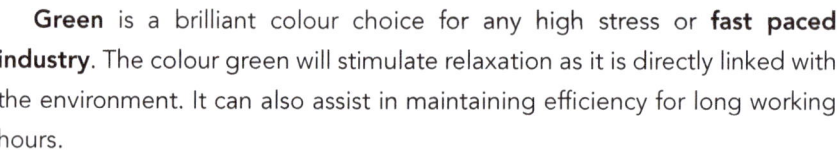

Green is a brilliant colour choice for any high stress or **fast paced industry**. The colour green will stimulate relaxation as it is directly linked with the environment. It can also assist in maintaining efficiency for long working hours.

Any work that requires **physical activity** would benefit from using the colour **red**. Red is wonderful for productivity, and can help increase heart rate and blood flow. Red may also evoke feelings of passion. Gyms or fitness centres would be smart to use red throughout.

THE COLOUR TO AVOID

There is one particular colour that should be avoided in all offices (which unfortunately still dominates many of them). Grey! Grey is passive, uninvolved, unmotivated, and lacks the energy required to be productive within any office space. It is a dull and uninspiring colour that I personally would not recommend. Using a lot of grey can create feelings of low confidence and even, in extreme cases, feelings of depression. A good way to avoid this is to eliminate grey completely. If you cannot do this, pair it with another colour to counter the low and dark feelings grey evokes.

You will know what kind of mood you want to create in your office. Take the time to choose the right colour for you, your staff and your customers.

Angela Wright, a world renowned colour psychologist, suggests that choosing the right colour shade and intensity is just as important as the colour itself. She says that, "What defines whether a colour is stimulating or soothing is not the colour, it's the intensity. A strong bright colour will stimulate, and a colour with low saturation will soothe."[1] This is something to keep in mind. Once you have chosen which colour you would like to focus your design around, consider the hues that you will incorporate. For example, will the colours be highly saturated (to stimulate) or more subdued (to soothe)?

THE RIGHT COLOUR SCHEME

Are you feeling overwhelmed by the thought of an entirely yellow or green office? It is a good idea to start with a neutral base colour (either a white or light grey) when creating your overall colour scheme. You can then build upon the base colour with other vibrant shades. Painting all of the walls in one solid, bright colour will become too overpowering and, depending on the colour, overstimulating. To create a perfect balance for the office, use light toned colours with splashes of your chosen colour scheme.

Your colour scheme may be significant to your brand or service. For example, children would feel more comfortable in a bright room than a plain one. So, if you were

DID YOU KNOW?

Colour extends past the physical office environment, and can be an important consideration in your office wear. For example, a blue suit worn to a business meeting will convey a good work ethic. However, a navy suit connotes authority and is a more suitable colour to wear when you want to look like the expert.

thinking of opening a doctor's practice, hospital, or childcare, you will want to include colours that would appeal to a child. Incorporating a decorative or feature wall using elements of different colours is another great way to liven up a space. You may even like to use artwork to highlight colours of your choice. Be as liberal and creative as you like.

If you are working with a fitout company that offer a design service, they will be able to guide you with colour choice, placement, and intensity.

ADD VIBRANCY TO YOUR OFFICE

Be adventurous and incorporate pops of colour throughout the office to add character and flair. Choose any shades you like to make it your own. Combining colours will create vibrancy and attitude, without overpowering the space. Give it a try to see what you can come up with!

EARTHY TONES WITH A HINT OF COLOUR

Earthy tones can get monotonous. Try adding a hint of colour throughout browns and greens to liven up your space. Add patterned wallpaper or bright furniture to bring attention to different places in the room.

A SENSORY JOURNEY   97

GET BOLD WITH RED, BLUE AND YELLOW

It can get a little scary using bold colours like red, blue and yellow. However, when used correctly, these shades will bring in the right amount of colour to build the atmosphere you want. Try painting just one side of a door or part of a wall a bold colour. You could even add in bright blue chairs paired with yellow pillows to spark imagination and creativity within the office.

GET THE RIGHT COLOUR SCHEME TO SUIT YOUR NEEDS

You should aim to use colours that match the theme of your business both in and around the office. At Future Fitouts, we have a dedicated team to help our clients choose the right colour palette. We ensure that colours blend together seamlessly to create the best representation of every brand.

Our first office was in an industrial shed. It was an awful beige filled with old off white and fawn coloured furniture. I am *convinced* that the space was not promoting a healthy feng shui, and was possibly even cursed (due to the amount of bad luck we had there)! We didn't realise how bad it was until we moved into our new 'Google inspired' office and noticed the substantial difference.

We made some bold moves in our new fitout and ended up incorporating brave and colourful statements throughout the space. We added bright lime green and cyan blue panels to the walls, with some areas covered in murals of the Brisbane cityscape. The windows were covered in spotted film and the floor was made up of brightly coloured carpet tiles. On paper it looked good, but both Aaron and I were hesitant in how it would work in real life.

The result = AMAZING!

It turned out better than we expected. Honestly, I could not have been happier! Since then, I have heard countless delivery drivers, consultants, clients, and visitors commenting on our office space. It is unbelievable! I am also happy that our team enjoys coming to work and being in the space every day.

Despite the distractions of an open plan office, I choose to work from the space as often as possible, rather than from my home office. The environment you create and colours you choose really do increase motivation and team productivity. This 'stuff' really works!

ARTWORK

Incorporating artwork into your design is completely your choice. If that is what you want to do, then go for it! After all, expensive artwork can be an investment. However, there is no need to fork out serious cash on pricey art if you don't want to. For as little as $20, you can find paintings and prints that will still add a splash of colour and freshen up your office.

There are many different types of art to choose from, including inspirational graphics, quotes, and photographs. If you are feeling creative yourself, you may like to try your own hand at painting an abstract artwork on a large canvas to put on display.

Showcase artwork that promotes the atmosphere you are trying to create. Just a small addition of art can bring a whole new feeling into the office and create the illusion of a new makeover at the same time.

I personally love relaxing murals placed at the end of a wall that transport you to another place or detailed signs that promote motivation and teamwork.

COLOURFUL TEXTILES

You might be surprised how fabulous your office can look by simply adding some colourful textiles. Making use of colour and textiles should not be underestimated. It is an affordable way to add more vibrancy to your space.

Consider adding an ornamental rug under the boardroom table, throwing some decorative pillows on the couch in your break out room, or hanging curtains with a unique design in the reception area. When picking colours for your textiles, refer to our guide on choosing the right colour scheme for your office to make sure you instil the right mood and encourage productivity. You can mix up the colour scheme when the mood strikes, or change the colours to match the seasons.

PLANTS

Do you have bare spaces and corners around your office? Why not fill them with plants!

There are many types of indoor plants you can purchase that will bring a little bit of the outdoors, indoors. Plants such as the Chinese evergreen, dracaena, calathea, or peace lily have the added benefit of producing oxygen, which can be a blessing to offices that lack natural ventilation and air flow. Alternatively, fake plants look great and do not require any maintenance (but obviously miss out on the oxygen benefits).

As well as adding some much needed life and greenery, a little bit of nature in the office has been shown to boost creativity. Nowadays, you can even find beautiful fake flowers that look so real, you will want to touch them.

FAKE VERSUS REAL PLANTS (HEALTH BENEFITS)

Real plants

Unlike fake plants, real plants require you to take care of them. You will need to make sure that they have enough water and are not in direct sunlight. Despite this, the benefits far outweigh the negatives. Incorporating real plants into your office space

will bring the outdoors, in. According to recent research, there are seven major benefits to bringing real plants into the office.[2]

- Plants help reduce stress.
- Plants help increase productivity in the office.
- Plants reduce sickness and rates of absenteeism.
- Plants make the office more attractive.
- Plants naturally clean the air.
- Plants help reduce noise levels.
- Plants boost creativity.

Having real plants at each desk or in the office has been proven to reduce stress by up to 60%.[3] *UP TO 60%!* Bring on more plants! 😊

Fake plants
Fake plants can still carry some of the same benefits of natural plants. They will make the office look more attractive, help reduce noise levels, and boost creativity. However, fake plants will not hold the natural benefits of real plants. For instance, they will not clean the air or create oxygen.

If you are unsure which way to go, one option would be to incorporate a mixture of real and fake plants in the office. You could place succulents and fake plants in areas that are more likely to be forgotten about, or do not offer proper light for plants to grow, and include real plants in brightly lit, common areas.

WORDS…POWERFUL (YET SUBTLE) MESSAGES

Visuals that motivate and inspire will always add value to your environment. Words are powerful to both our conscious and subconscious. (We are always working on a subconscious level to some degree.)

Our office has words, signs, and positive quotes scattered throughout. When you enter the Future Fitouts space, the first thing you see on the front door is a sign that reads "Welcome to the Future Fitouts Family." This small but powerful message instantly creates a sense of welcoming and acceptance to everyone who enters the office. It also shows our team that they are part of our family and that we care about them.

Have you ever been invited to someone's house and they are so hospitable that it feels like you are in your own family home? You feel welcome to help yourself to the contents of the fridge, grab your own drinks, and make yourself comfortable. Think about how you can create this sentiment in your workplace.

The second sign delivering a subtle message is located strategically up the stairs leading into the office. This sign reads, "Bring your Best Self." It is lit up in a neon light and placed on a fake plant green wall. The wording, colours and placement all contribute to delivering a positive message to all who enter the space.

Every person who walks into the office reads this sign, even if they are unaware of it. Instantly, they make a subtle adjustment to their mood, subconsciously choosing their attitude for the day.

Finally, in the waiting area where our boardroom is situated, we have four words etched across the sliding doors: "Great Minds Think Alike." This contains another subliminal message to anyone who enters the boardroom: we are here to discuss big ideas, and strong minds are at work. This signage has been strategically placed and carefully chosen to make a big impact.

Along with inspiring words that anyone can identify with, it is important to bring out the individual passions and motivations of each team member to show that they matter. I will discuss this further in the next part of the book.

GOALS AND VISION BOARDS

You may have heard of the famous self-help book and film *The Secret* by Rhonda Byrne. If you haven't, grab yourself a copy. *The Secret* discusses the law of attraction and how you can use it to better your life. One technique Rhonda suggests is creating a dream or vision board to manifest and attract everything you want.

I love this concept, and have done so from a very young age. I have always had a vision board in my room with magazine cut outs or printed images of the things that I would like to achieve. I get huge satisfaction from ticking things off and seeing the vision board become a reality.

I brought this idea into the workplace many years ago by dedicating a wall in the office to display our team's individual goals – our 'Goal Board'. Of course, the location of the Goal Board was a strategic decision. Can you guess its location?

What area has the heaviest foot traffic and is used multiple times a day by all staff members?

The printer!

This is my favourite part of our entire office. The wall above the printer is now covered with pictures of what our team wants to achieve, including small and big goals, long and short term. (If you are wondering, writing a book was one of my goals and is now ticked off. *YES!*)

The wall is fascinating to look at and is a constant reminder of everyone's ambitions. It also shows the team that we are here to support one another in achieving both professional and – more importantly – personal goals. The goal wall engages our team by showing them that we genuinely care about

> **Your should set goals beyond your reach so you always have something to live for."**
> **– Ted Turner**

their personal achievements. At Future Fitouts, we take this one step further and spend time working with each staff member on their individual goals and formulate a plan to achieve them.

POSITIVE AND PERSONALISED SPACES

When creating a positive space, it is a rule of thumb to get rid of anything that is outdated or, as Marie Kondo famously says, does not "spark joy." If you are unsure what to keep and what to bin, start by collecting the things you enjoy and make you feel happy. What's left over? Does it deserve a place in your space? You want to create an environment that reflects your culture and is inviting to all who enter it. Play around with ideas, google some inspirational images, and take your time to create your personalised space.

Allowing team members to personalise their desks (and team environment) is a great start. I have walked into offices and immediately sensed the team dynamics and culture that has been embedded. I recall one space where the team members had a dedicated 'travel wall'. This wall was centred by a world map with pins marking where each employee had been. Around the map were photos, postcards, and a countdown to trips that employees had booked in. It was a real talking point for the staff and created a strong bond between them. Another office collected snow globes from when their employees visited other countries.

You might like to display other exciting news and share it around the team, such as new baby arrivals, birthdays, special days, and events that you can all celebrate together to feel like part of a family. You might also like to try something fun, like recreating the awkward family Christmas photo together.

COMPANY DASHBOARDS

Engaging your team by displaying company KPIs and showing progress towards goals is an excellent way to increase motivation and build team morale! There are some incredibly sophisticated dashboards out there that can track team progress. I have seen some that play a team anthem (*really* loudly) once a deal has been finalised, and others that display team leader boards to create healthy competition between similar roles and departments. There are some excellent online platforms available to build dashboards easily and quickly.

STATIONERY AND OFFICE SUPPLIES

Don't settle for boring, run of the mill stationery – bring some flair to the office with funky desk accessories! It is something so simple that can bring *a lot* of excitement to the office.

Upgrade your office supplies to reflect the theme of your space. Bright mouse pads, geometric pen holders, and branded notepads are small additions that can really make your space pop. Hanging a vibrant desk calendar in each workstation is another simple way to incorporate colour into an otherwise dull area (and also has the added benefit of keeping your team organised).

There are many shops that sell designer stationery sets. Alternatively, head online to sites like Snap or Vistaprint to customise your own office stationery. You could even try your hand at creating some DIY notepads or cubicle decorations yourself!

Sound

THE POWER OF SOUND!

This is one of my favourite elements to play with when creating a space.

Now, when I talk about sound, I am not referring to a white noise tape filled with sounds of frantic keyboard typing, phones ringing, and the shuffling of papers (though some people do work well to this).

People work differently. If you are going to play sound or music in your office, it is important to consider the type of mood it will create and whether it will become a distraction, rather than a motivation.

Picture yourself walking into a gym with the objective to train hard. If soft classical music was playing, you probably wouldn't feel very motivated to work out, would you? However, if the gym was playing loud, fast paced music, you would be more likely to feel driven to smash your workout.

It is important to keep this concept in mind when selecting the sounds in your office. Key word: *selecting*. You must choose exactly what is played in your space. At Future Fitouts, we have carefully selected the background music that plays in common areas. Many of our employees also work with headphones.

Headphones allow individuals to choose their own music to get into a flow and peaceful state of mind. Also, headphones are a great visual prompt to indicate that other colleagues not to interrupt. It subtly says, "I am in the middle of doing something, please don't bother me." This reduces the number of distractions and increases output.

We have also recently introduced 'stop signs' that team members can display above their screens if they are really trying to focus on a task without distraction.

You may also like to incorporate fun signs like the one below to add humour into your space.

At Future Fitouts, we have installed several speakers around

the office that play internet radio stations with limited or no ads. We stay away from mainstream radio stations, because after a couple of songs either a (generally negative) news update or annoying ad will interrupt and distract the team.

Choosing specific sounds has been scientifically proven. Type 'best music for studying' into an internet search and you will see pages and pages of results filled with research backed evidence from universities, professors, and scientists. When you allow the music to just 'be' in the office and turn on mainstream radio, you could actually be killing motivation or creating a depressive state without even knowing it. Not to mention, your team will start to comment that they have heard the same song five times that day.

So, while you are rushing to turn off all the radios, what can you do instead?

It pays to have the right kind of music playing in the workplace. Future Fitouts incorporates music into the office with a frequency of **432 Hz and 528 Hz**. These two frequencies resonate in cosmic harmony, and many believe they create healing vibrations for the mind, body, and spirit. We choose these channels when the noise level is getting too loud and the change of music instantly calms the team down.

432 Hz sounds are considered to heighten perception and increase mental clarity. This is important if you are using sound to help increase productivity and maintain happier staff. 528 Hz has been shown to repair damaged DNA (but that is a matter for the scientists). How different frequencies affect our state of mind might be something you are interested in learning more about. For now, I just wanted to make a brief mention so that you are aware sounds have an impact on learning and cognition.

There are apps you can download that tell you the frequency of the music you are listening to. Usually a tuner will also tell you the frequency of a sound.

Of course, on Friday afternoons we get the party mix playing to bring out the fun within the team!

SOUNDS OF CELEBRATIONS

A key way you can create and cultivate culture in your workplace is to celebrate wins and milestones. What better way to do this than through sound? At Future Fitouts, we have done just that by incorporating an auditory ritual to acknowledge success.

For us, we wanted something loud that had a deeper meaning or spiritual element to it. After some research, we discovered that traditional Balinese gongs have been used for thousands of years in sacred ceremonies and celebrations.

After months of searching and testing gongs (we were very particular) we came across a beautiful gong that had been handmade in Bali.

The gong now sits proudly in our office corner in the 'celebration zone'. It is such a pleasurable sound and the

noise gives everyone goose bumps. The power and vibration of the gong is a form of therapy. When it is struck in celebration, it echoes throughout the building and lifts the mood of the office.

We hit the gong as often as possible and take the time to really stop and celebrate with the team (even if it is only for a few minutes). We hit the gong every time we win a new contract, complete a project, reach a personal goal or company milestone, and to celebrate birthdays and awards. It is the best feeling when a team member gets up, casually walks over to the gong and gives it a big whack. The entire team stops to clap, cheer, and celebrate.

As I grew more interested in the power of these traditional gongs and continued learning about them, I eventually came across a practice called gong healing. Using my team as a guinea pig (they have become used to my crazy ideas), we invited a gong meditation practitioner into our office during our busiest and most stressful time to perform a gong meditation session. The benefits were unbelievable! Our employees became more relaxed, productive and focused and were less stressed after just one one hour session. This is something we have since incorporated into our yearly calendar.

If this interests you, I have included a sample gong mediation and further information in the Interactive Book.

HOW DO YOU CELEBRATE WITH YOUR TEAM?

Creating an area for celebration is key when building office culture. Think about when a sports team wins a game. It is always followed by a celebration where players, supporters, and fans revel in the victory. Imagine that your staff are part of a sporting team. How can you celebrate their wins?

As busy business owners, I understand that there is never enough time in the day. We just keep working and pushing through to get things done. However, celebrating is important. It is the small recognitions that build a strong, high performing team. Not every celebration has to cost time, money, and excursions out of the office (though these are important too). There are many easy ways that you can celebrate the wins within your team on a daily basis.

You don't have to use a gong, but could try sounding a bell, buzzer, or team song to acknowledge a small win. Alternatively, donating to charity (read more about B1G1 later in this book), starting a round of applause, playing a quick game of ping pong, or giving high-fives around the office are simple and effortless ways you can show appreciation for your staff.

Write down a few ideas you can implement into your team right now and then share them with me through my interactive book.

_____

_____

_____

_____

_____

_____

_____

_____

_____

_____

_____

Smell

> **❝** *Nothing brings to life again a forgotten memory like a fragrance."*
> *– Christopher Poindexter*

These days, everywhere you look, someone is selling candles or essential oils (or both). Diffusing essential oils is my first choice for the office. It is a little safer, as you don't have to remember to blow out a candle at the end of the day, and the scent can be changed as often as you like.

ESSENTIAL OILS

Have you ever smelled something that makes you feel instantly nostalgic? Perhaps the scent of freshly baked bread takes you back to your childhood, or a specific aftershave reminds you of your father. This is because the brain's emotional response to smell is linked to fear, pleasure, and motivation. Smell can also impact memory and learning.

Tap into this and use it to your advantage in the workplace. By appropriately manipulating smells within the office, you can promote focus, mental clarity, and memory. For example, peppermint scented oils can enhance alertness, focus, concentration, and the accuracy of memory.[4]

According to the *American College of Healthcare Sciences*, some of the best scents to incorporate into the office include rosemary, bergamot, geranium, lemongrass and clove.[5] (Lemongrass and wild orange are our top picks at Future Fitouts.)

Rosemary has been found to increase memory, concentration, and alertness, and can also assist in solving problems faster.[6] Scents like bergamot and geranium can be used as a mood booster, while lemongrass can increase awareness and energy.[7]

Using the right essential oils can also positively affect children with ADHD. For example, in a study by Dr Terry Friedmann, children who were exposed to and inhaled the vetiver essential oil experienced an improvement in brain patterns and decreased ADHD symptoms.[8]

A study in Japan has also found that aromatherapy can improve cognitive function and the ability to form abstract ideas in dementia patients. In the study, the group were exposed to rosemary, lemon, lavender and orange essential oils, which were shown to have positive effects.[9]

> *If you want a productive workspace and team, try out some oils and benefit your business with the power of smell! Why not take it one step further and create a signature brand scent that clients can associate with your business!*

Taste

WELL FED AND HAPPY TEAM

Good food makes us all happy, so taste is an essential consideration when building your office culture. Everyone loves a reward for a job well done (or just as a thank you for the work they do) and **one of the best, easiest, and most appreciated incentives is food**.

Providing a selection of healthy and unhealthy treats is always appreciated within a team. Make sure that you have staple foods on hand, like crackers and condiments, biscuits, and mints that your staff can help themselves to. Organising a weekly fresh fruit delivery is another great way you can give your team a healthy boost that they can look forward to.

You can also create surprises as a small gesture of appreciation for your staff, such as handing out coffee vouchers or bringing in coffees for the team. A great idea is to organise a coffee van to attend your site and prepay for everyone's order. Alternatively, you could try some of the suggestions below.

- Stock the freezer with smoothie packets so that staff can whip up a fruity drink for themselves.

- Surprise your team with boxes of ice blocks on a hot day.

- Buy up on toppings, nuts, marshmallows, and ice cream and make sundaes for your team.

- If you have an oven in the office, keep frozen snacks (pies, sausage rolls and pastries) on hand for Friday afternoon wind downs.

- Provide staff with cake and bakery treats. (Enough said.)

- Leave a chocolate or small treat on everyone's desk with a thank you note.

- Order pizza to the office after meeting a deadline or handing over a successful project.

- Have muesli bars and cereal on hand.

- Keep a supply of nuts, fruits and healthy options in the kitchen in fancy jars so that your team can help themselves.

- Provide drinks to staff. These don't need to be alcoholic. Stock the fridge with kombucha, coconut water, soft drinks, and mineral waters for staff to take as they wish.

Random gestures of appreciation will greatly impact productivity. Your staff will feel valued and go above and beyond for you and the company. This, in turn, boosts morale and team spirit. (Be mindful that too many carb filled treats can leave your staff feeling lethargic and unmotivated. But as a random surprise, it's totally worth it!)

BRINGING YOUR TEAM TOGETHER WITH FOOD

Building social connections within the team is an important element to having a happy and uplifting office space. Do your staff feel like they have to eat at their desks? Or, do you have an area where everyone can sit together and mingle? It is a good idea to create a space where people feel that they can be social, away from their desks, when they have lunch. Your staff should feel that they have had a proper break, so that when they return to their work for the afternoon they are rested and relaxed.

Eating together will also create a culture of family and togetherness in your office. You may like to schedule a set lunch time where everyone breaks together, or provide an open space where people can choose to come and go as they please.

Whether you throw Friday drinks and nibbles, team lunches, or birthday celebrations, food will always bring people together!

TIME FOR A COFFEE BREAK

I get it. You have read a few chapters and need a break. But literally *having organised coffee breaks is a science backed idea to boost productivity in the work place.*

Productivity is a major concern for managers across the world. This has undoubtedly been heightened by the general loss of the old-fashioned nine-to-five, cubicle based working environment. Many employees no longer have (or want) the same rigid structures of the past, and expect some flexibility in their working patterns. While this shift away from strict working conditions is keeping employees satisfied, it is causing managers to break out in a cold sweat!

Flexibility naturally poses a risk to productivity, and it is safe to say that there has never been more emphasis on efficiency and output than there is today. Managers are constantly thinking up ways that they can better motivate staff, maximise production, and reduce the number of unproductive tasks completed during working hours. Some employers go so far as restricting web use or banning personal devices. Others cut out coffee breaks and other non-work related activities. But is this really what's best for employees, or

> Face-to-face conversation is equal to 34 emails

do these kinds of restrictions just create a culture of control and inhibit creativity?

You need to look at both sides of the coin when considering how best to maximise output. Is forcing the idea of productivity really the best way to succeed? Or, would it be more beneficial to back off a little and give your staff the space to work in a way that best suits them? By pushing your employees, are you doing more harm than good?

Often, the focus is placed on *how often* employees work, rather than *how* they work. Boosting productivity in the workplace is not about working longer or working harder, it is about working smarter and making better choices.

THE IMPORTANCE OF THE COFFEE BREAK

Experts claim that regular coffee breaks boost productivity and are essential for peak performance in the workplace. While the concept of doing less work to achieve more may sound strange, the reasoning is pretty solid. By resting the brain, we are able to take a step back and see things more clearly. 'Shower thoughts' are a prime example of this. Think about it. Have you ever had a genius idea in the shower? Or thought up a solution to your problems while you're out for a run? Sometimes, we need to take a step back in order to view the situation with more clarity.

A coffee break alone is not enough. Boosting productivity isn't just about the existence of coffee breaks. It is about how these breaks are organised; when they are taken, how often they are taken, and who they are taken with. Scheduling organised coffee breaks is a great way to boost productivity.

THE ORGANISED COFFEE BREAK: HOW, WHEN, AND WITH WHOM

Quite simply, a random approach to coffee breaks just isn't going to cut it. In fact, it could actually do more harm than good and encourage sloppy working patterns. Instead, it is best to organise workplace coffee breaks to ensure that all employees are getting the most from their rests.

Here are some aspects to take into consideration:

Coffee with friends
Enjoying a coffee with friends, rather than alone, can help to reinforce workplace friendships and improve the strength of office social groups.

Employees who are a part of a strong workplace community typically show higher levels of productivity than those who spend time alone.

The rule of 52 and 17

The most productive employees work for an average of 52 minutes at a time, with a 17 minute break in between periods of working. Experts claim that 17 minutes is long enough to completely remove yourself from your workload, returning with a clear head and more energy.

Other studies show that an average adult can only focus for 6 minutes without a distraction or interruption from an external source (usually an email, app notification, team interruption or phone call).

AM v PM

Coffee breaks become less beneficial as the day goes on. It is easier to restore energy in the morning when levels are high, rather than later in the day when they naturally deplete.

Why coffee?

Of course, the term 'coffee break' is just a name. It does not necessarily refer to the beverage itself, but rather a rest period during working hours.

In saying that, let's think about coffee in terms of productivity. It is reported that happy employees are 12% more productive than their unhappy counterparts, and there is perhaps no other beverage that makes us feel quite so thrilled as a big cuppa joe (and this is coming from someone who has never had a cup of coffee in her life)!

There is a biological reason for this. Coffee is understood to stimulate the production and release of a chemical called dopamine, which makes us experience feelings of euphoria. Caffeinated teas, which help to keep us alert, are also good options to generate similar effects.

> *You cannot mandate productivity; you must provide the tools to let people become their best."*
> *– Steve Jobs*

Your next step

If you are concerned about productivity in the office, there are a number of things you can do to create a more focussed environment. Providing staff with additional training, or introducing timesheets to track work flow and analyse data are great places to start. You could also try downloading creative phone applications to help employees stay on task and resist phone addictions. For example, *Forest*, an app by development team Seekrtech, helps the user abstain from phone use by awarding credits so that real trees can be planted around the world. The longer the user stays focused, the bigger their forest grows.

TIP

Did you know that an employee working across two monitors, instead of one, can increase their productivity by 20% to 30%?[10]
Spend extra on a larger screen with high resolution – it really will make a difference!

Touch

Touch is an interesting concept in the workplace. It is the first sense we form as humans and is a powerful non-verbal signal of our emotions. (Think about what a simple handshake can tell you about someone.)

However, this section is not about physical connection with others at work (see Part Six, 'Showing Love at Work' for more on this). In this section, we will explore how the sense of touch can be stimulated appropriately in the office through your fitout.

TEXTURES AND TEXTILES

Incorporating different tactile materials into the office can excite, inspire, stimulate, calm, and nurture your staff and clients. For example, using soft furnishings in your space, such as a thick plush rug or a comfortable couch, can mimic a home environment and promote feelings of comfort and security.

You will find that your team's mental health and productivity will benefit greatly from having access to areas that encourage relaxation and allow them to switch off and get away from their desks for a while. You may find that some people like to slouch on a soft, cushion filled sofa while talking on the phone or working on a laptop. Having options like this are crucial for your team's wellbeing.

Another great way to stimulate the sense of touch in the office is to provide staff with individual back rollers, so that they can massage themselves while sitting at their desks. Some workplaces have even opted for entire massage walls, where employees can squat and roll their spines over rollers that have been installed across the façade. Both options relieve stress and tension in back muscles and will leave your team feeling reinvigorated.

Humans are very dependent on meaningful contact. Depending on the type of environment you want to foster, you could incorporate a hug corner or a stretch zone into your fitout plans. Both of these can help you feel better during a long day at work.

THINK OUTSIDE THE OFFICE CHAIR

Some people need to touch or feel things in order to understand them. These people learn by 'doing' things (rather than reading how to do them, or watching someone else do them). This is known as tactile or kinaesthetic learning. Placing a tray of mind puzzles or games in meeting rooms is a great way to enhance the **sensory journey for everyone, and will also give tactile learners an area to escape to**.

I once noticed that there was a random piece of felt fabric on my colleague's desk. I assumed that it was a project sample, so I put it away. She stopped me, and said that one of the designers gave it to her to use as a 'stress pad' to help her calm down. When things got too busy and tense, she touched the fabric and it would bring her back to the present moment.

This was such a beautiful idea and thoughtful gift. (I also felt very happy to have a team that genuinely cared about one another. This is the culture I am speaking of!)

Switching out office chairs for Swiss balls is another way that your team can explore touch in the office. You could even designate a small area to stretch and yoga by filling it with exercise balls and yoga mats. (Reiki or yoga mats could also be a good option for lining desk chairs to give relief to back tension. The ideas are endless!)

Implementing Your Sensory Experience

PUTTING IT ALL TOGETHER

We all want to work in an environment that is comfortable, uplifting, and inspiring. However, if you aren't ready or don't have the budget for a complete office fitout, implementing just some of these low cost, sensory experiences will make all the difference to your workplace and improve motivation. Sometimes it's the simple things that make the biggest difference!

FENG SHUI

Feng shui is the ancient Chinese practice of arranging interactions between people and their environments through careful and considered design and management of a space. Feng shui is used to balance the energy of rooms, offices, and homes around the world to provide comfort, harmony, and a positive energy for people living and working in these spaces.

I have outlined some things you may like to consider when creating a positive energy flow below.

You may also like to hire a feng shui professional who can come into your space and help you out.

LAYOUT

Think about how the space is set up. Look at where fixed elements (doors, walls, and windows) are located and how the furniture is arranged. Does anything feel 'off' when you look at the space?

Traditionally in a feng shui office, desks should be positioned facing the door, so that the worker can see who is coming and going from their office. Try moving furniture around to achieve this. If this is not possible, place a mirror on the desk so that the team member can see behind them.

If you have the space, set aside an area – even a corner of the office – that invites your staff to meditate or take time out when things get stressful. Creating a zone where staff can switch off during work hours will do wonders for their mood, productivity, and mental health.

Let your intuition guide you and feel free to experiment with as many different layouts as you like.

IT'S TIME FOR A SPRING CLEAN!

Remember those memos you stashed in your desk drawer because you just 'haven't gotten around to filing them yet'? Or the half empty packets of gum sitting next to your computer monitor 'just in case' a client pops in for a quick chat? Get. Rid. Of. Them!

Anything that is not essential to your workspace needs to go. That includes rubbish, personal items, broken furniture and empty boxes. Providing a clean and open workspace is critical in keeping you and your staff focused and relaxed.

It is a good idea to get into the habit of decluttering your space regularly so that you do not feel overwhelmed. Tidy all drawers, desks, bins, cupboards, shelves and filing cabinets. Check individual workstations, as well as communal areas like meeting rooms and kitchens for items that need to be discarded. The number of plastic containers that can accumulate on a drying rack in the kitchen never ceases to amaze me!

Reduce digital clutter by removing surplus icons from your computer desktop and organising your soft copy files. Clean up your calendar to give yourself a clear visual of your upcoming commitments.

Is it possible for your office to go paperless? If so, this is a great idea to reduce unnecessary paper, printer, and file storage clutter. Working from cloud based systems also has the added benefit of staff being able to access anything they require remotely. This would give you the option to declutter the space by removing the workstations of staff who do not work from the office.

LIGHTING

Take advantage of any natural light that your space has access to by using a layout that allows light to filter through the office. This will uplift team members and help combat fatigue.

If, like most offices, you are largely relying on artificial light, invest in globes that emulate natural light. Try not to use fluorescent lights that drain your energy (and power bill).

CLEAN AIR MEANS CLEAN THOUGHTS

There is nothing worse than sitting in a stuffy, hot office. If your office does not have windows that open, consider introducing desk fans, a small water fountain, an air purifier, or a fish tank. These small items will allow the air to flow more efficiently through the office. Fresh flowers and greenery will also open the space.

COLOURS AND ARTWORK

Choose colours and artwork that make you feel inspired. (Flick back to 'Sight' on page 91 for more on this.)

CREATE A HEALTHY OFFICE HABIT

It is important to get in the habit of maintaining your space. Create a schedule so that your staff understand what they are responsible for, such as watering the plants or feeding the fish. Rotating these little jobs will also promote a homely feel.

A clean environment means healthy employees and happy people all round. Remember, we spend more time at work than in our own homes!

LET YOUR INTUITION GUIDE YOU

There is no hard and fast rule that applies to everyone. Look around you and see what *feels* off and change it. This is the most important aspect to feng shui. Feng shui is about making your work space more inspiring and calm for you, your staff and your clients. Surround yourself with what you love to bring in inspiration and motivation.

I am by no means an expert in this field, but if feng shui inspires you and you want to learn more, there are many resources for you to read and look at. Hiring a feng shui expert could also be beneficial if this sparks your interest.

CREATE YOUR SENSORY CHECKLIST HERE

CREATE YOUR SENSORY CHECKLIST HERE

PART FOUR

BUILD SYSTEMS FOR SUCCESS

(Positive minds think alike!)

The Benefits of S.Y.S.T.E.M.S

This is one of my favourite topics. I could quite literally write an entire book on systems and how they increase business efficiency. I *love* creating business systems and I am always looking at every process to see how we can improve it.

However, for the purpose of keeping this book a reasonable size, I will take you through just a few key systems and explain how they can benefit your business.

When you break down the word 'systems', it becomes an acronym (and a very useful one).

Save **Y**our **S**elf **T**ime **E**nergy **M**oney & **S**tress

WHAT DOES THIS MEAN?

When you are a business owner, you have a lot on your plate. You wear multiple hats and assume various roles just so that you can get your business off the ground. You are the marketing, accounts, delivery, IT, sales, after service, and human resources department. Literally everything rests on your shoulders!

This is necessary in the short term, but eventually, will become unsustainable and can be a cause of burnout. Your business will grow, rendering you unable to complete every task on your own. The natural and most common thing to do at this stage is to start bringing on more people in the hope they will relieve some of the workload.

You do this. But instead of working *less*, you now find yourself doing more and more – working extra hours, longer days and spending additional time answering questions. You feel stuck, exhausted, and often wonder what the whole point of bringing on people was, if not to reduce your workload and stress. You are wondering if things are being completed the same way you do them or the way you want them to be done. This is where systems come in.

Systems are created to ensure uniformity across all areas of your business and will help save you time, money, energy and stress. Every task (big or small) within your business has a specific way that it should be done. These processes need to be recorded (and kept updated) in a user friendly system. By recording instructions for each job, you (and others in your team) will be able to quickly train staff on how the task should be completed.

> How does a 15 year old working at McDonalds make the same tasting burger anywhere around the world in less than 180 seconds?[1] SYSTEMS!

Systems come in many different forms – procedures, policies, guidelines, checklists, reference tools, training videos, quality checks, templates and production lines. Any process that is time saving and creates efficiency is a system.

Running a construction company with many moving parts (managing numerous roles, subcontractors, timeframes) and delivering over 100 projects a year, I have managed to systemise our business into three core categories: new enquiry, job won, and job complete.

While there are a large number of tasks within each category, Aaron and I have been able to keep our overheads down and staff numbers low by creating a uniform way of doing things. This ensures that we achieve consistency with our clients every single time (it doesn't matter who is looking after the project or if a team member leaves, the process of delivery is done the 'Future Fitouts Way'). Every team member is involved in every project and has an important part to play. These systems also hold each person accountable for the outcome.

WHERE TO START

Creating systems can be time consuming upfront, and if you are not naturally 'system minded' it pays to get a professional in to help you. Investing in systems will pay itself back time and time again. The right systems will reduce staff costs, overheads, and minimise mistakes and reworks.

The systems required will vary depending on the size and stage of your business. For example, at the startup stage, you will be lucky to have any systems in place at all. The more mature the business is, you may find that there are a number of outdated or obsolete systems and processes that can be refined and improved.

I remember the very first system I created at Future Fitouts. The only staff were Aaron and I, and I spent an incredible amount of time developing our file/folder structure. It sounds so simple, but it took me *ages* to get it right (I was thinking long term about how the folder structure would work when we eventually hired staff and teams). Eleven years on and that same structure is still in place today (with some minor tweaks here and there, of course).

Over the years, I have been told various information about the best ways to make systems. I have created extremely detailed systems that outline each step of the process (I'm talking a three page process with particulars like "use a black pen" and "include a 3 cm block of Blu Tack" detailed), through to high-level guidelines (one page summaries) that focus on an outcome and allow others to determine the best way to achieve it.

TASK: HOW TO CREATE AND SEND AN INVOICE

	PROS
DETAILED SYSTEMS	<ul><li>Anyone with any level of experience (or no experience) can follow the system.</li><li>The task is done exactly the same each and every time.</li><li>It is easy to correct mistakes and is an excellent tool for training team members.</li><li>Good for important tasks.</li></ul>
OUTCOME BASED SYSTEMS	<ul><li>Focuses on the (often more important) outcome rather than the detail.</li><li>Gives the team greater control over how the task is performed.</li><li>Individuals can find the most efficient way to complete the task.</li><li>Business owners know the outcome is being achieved, even if the way of achieving it takes a different path.</li></ul>

My advice is: it depends on the task and the importance of 'completing it to the letter' as to how much detail is provided. Using the example above, if a blue (instead of black) pen is used and the Blu Tack has not been measured to 3 cm *but* the site folder is created within 24 hours, the outcome has been achieved and is therefore more important than the colour of pen.

Systems should not become overcomplicated and businesses should have a variety of systems to suit different learning styles. The easiest way to do this is to start with an outcome based system, then combine the detailed steps as required. Try to keep it to one page and always refer to role titles, as opposed to employee names. If a system is too complex, break it down into separate parts.

Consider what level of detail is critical to the task you are trying to document to determine whether you should create a detailed or outcome based system. There are pros and cons of each, per the quick summary table below.

CONS	EXAMPLES OF SYSTEM TYPE
o Very time consuming to create. o Some staff might feel micromanaged. o Does not encourage problem solving/ independent thinking. o Creates an expectation that all systems should be the same.	o Email templates o Video training o Detailed work instructions and operating procedures o Checklists and verification processes System: Video training showing how invoices are created with detailed steps. Creation of email templates and specific checklists. The system is very clearly documented, leaving no ambiguity for the user.
o Each team member might achieve the outcome differently. o Staff might make assumptions or raise questions about the task. o The most efficient way of doing the task might never be recorded.	o Tasks linked to individual and team key performance indicators (KPIs) and key performance objectives (KPOs) o Guidelines and framework o High-level policies System: It is company policy for the accounts team to send invoices within five days using accounting software. Invoices over $5,000 to be checked by the manager.

Let's start creating our first system.

To begin, write a list of all the systems you want to create. Prioritise them by considering the below two questions.

1. What is the biggest point of pain within your business right now?

2. Which tasks do you no longer want to complete yourself?

Always focus on fixing the biggest pain point or problem first. Think about what isn't working or what could be done better in your business.

Map out how this task should be completed. Outline the key steps, how should be performed, by who, and in what time frame (if applicable). Then, write it down.

Congratulations, you have created your first system!

Formalise this by creating a system database, either in hard copy or online (we use SharePoint pages to store our systems as they are very easy to update and can hyperlink to other places). I have provided an easy template for you to use on page 132.

Then, follow the same process but for the task that is next highest in priority. Eventually, you will work your way down the list and every task and responsibility will have a process to follow. If you already have staff, have them compile a list of their tasks and document how they complete them. Ask them to write a system for everything they do and set key performance indicators to ensure it is completed to standard.

Answer these simple questions to start building your own systems!

1. **What problem are we trying to solve?**

   Are we trying to save time, minimise mistakes, improve efficiency, train staff,

TIP

Aim to create two systems per week. That will give you 104 systems a year!

better client retention and user experience, or create new processes? Are we trying to solve something more complicated?

2. **Why do we need this system?**

   If this is a new system, why are we creating it? If it is an existing system, why is it needed? Does this system serve a purpose?

3. **How can we do this better?**

   Can we simplify this process? What small improvements can we make today that would make this system more beneficial? Can we make it 1% better?

4. **Who is this system for?**

   Who is the end user? Who will be assigned to creating this system, testing it and updating it? Do we need to outsource this system or can we build it in house?

5. **When do we need this system?**

   Knowing your deadline will assist in holding people accountable so that the system can be implemented as soon as possible.

SYSTEMISE EVERYTHING

When our business coach first told us that we had to systemise everything, I thought he was crazy! "Why would I spend so much time systemising the small stuff? Shouldn't some things just be common sense?"

He shared an example to prove that even the most mundane jobs needed a process to follow. Our coach had a client who complained about staff members leaving lights on after they had left the office. When the client asked our coach what to do about it, he replied, "yes, turning lights off is simple, but unless staff are told there is a system to follow, they will not know how to complete it or whether it is their responsibility to do so. The staff may have assumed that leaving the lights on was the right thing to do, from a security perspective."

He told the client to create a FILO (First In, Last Out) system and stick the instructions above the light switch. This explained the process for locking up, and that the responsibility of doing so lay with whoever was the last to leave. It was never an issue again. This is one very simple example of how systems create structure, routine and a process for all to follow.

As mentioned already, I love systems! It makes training new team members a breeze, guarantees consistency throughout the organisation, and means that I don't have to remember everything that is going on. Plus, there are some tasks that only need to be completed annually. Because I have mapped out the process for these, I don't need to waste time relearning how to do them, or worrying about missing crucial steps.

SYSTEMS AND CULTURE

Systems can help create and maintain the **culture** of a company by allowing business owners to step away from the day-to-day. It is no longer "this is how Lauren runs the business" or "this is how the manager wants things done." The terminology starts to change. It becomes, "this is the Future Fitouts Way" or "this is how the company does it." This will also make it a lot easier to discuss performance with underachieving employees, as you can explain that they are not meeting the *company's* standard (rather than your own personal expectations).

If you are in the early stages of your business, success and freedom will come sooner if you start implementing systems now. Ask yourself which tasks you don't want to be doing all the time and what areas of the business you eventually want to hand over. You need to consider a long-term strategy (particularly if you don't have many, or any, staff). This is the basis of how systems are formed.

For now, it really doesn't matter what stage your business is at. Systems will always improve performance, guarantee consistency, increase profitability, provide clear reporting, and create freedom.

As your business evolves, so will your systems. Constantly review and update your systems to ensure that everything is being completed in the most efficient way. Alter and improve any systems that are not working for your business.

SYSTEMS DON'T NEED TO BE COMPLICATED

Steve Jobs had a vision that all Apple products be simple and easy to use.

He was known for his sleek and simplified designs. The products, packaging, store layouts, colours, and logo were all designed to be uniform. Even the 'iProduct' naming protocol created a simple and consistent name for future products. This was all part of his overall vision.

I have spent countless hours writing and perfecting our business systems. I am still working on them, as good systems are continually refined to reflect updated processes, changes, and improvements. The systems we have in place have paved our way to success and saved us huge amounts of money and time along the way. You only have to write a system once for it to be used over and over again.

The time we spent in the early days constructing our systems has paid off time and time again. Aaron and I can now enjoy a break through the week, or better yet, take an entire weekend off work. We can go away for a long weekend every once in a while and have more freedom now than ever before. This is because we have trust in our systems and know that they are working for us.

Do yourself a favour. Save Your Self Time Energy, Money and Stress and systemise EVERYTHING you can (or hire someone to do it for you)!

Just a word of caution: avoid *over* systemising. You don't want people to become so reliant on systems that they stop thinking for themselves.

EXAMPLE SYSTEM FRAMEWORK

Complete the template on the following page to create your first system. Fill out the top half (coloured in green) yourself (this is the what, why, how, and when) Then, ask your staff (if you have them) to complete the detailed steps (in blue).

QUICK SYSTEM WINS

Systems create routine, structure, consistency, quality, and are a management tool for performance. They are also great when onboarding new employees into your team and culture.

As a very small starting guide, a few systems that your business might need are listed on the next page. I have left space for you to fill in any systems that spring to mind when considering your own business.

(WHAT IS THE SYSTEM?)

Procedure Name:

- Create and Send Invoices

(WHY DO WE DO IT?)

Policy/Outcome:

- It is [company name's] policy to send invoices within five days of each month using the accounting software.

(WHO DOES IT?)

Who is Responsible:

- Accounts Team

(WHAT RESOURCES ARE NEEDED?)

Resources/Systems:

- Accounting software platform
- Link to video training

(HOW DO WE KNOW IT'S DONE RIGHT?)

Verification and Checks:

- Invoices over $5,000 to be checked by Manager

(WHEN IS IT DONE?)

Timeframe:

- 25th of every month

(DETAIL)

1. Open the accounting software.
2. Click on 'invoices'.
3. Enter new customer (link to Create New Customer system here).
4. Enter the invoice amount, date and other payment terms.
5. List any taxes.
6. Save to file.
7. Email to client.

(RELATED SYSTEMS)

Link to related systems here.

SYSTEMS CHECKLIST

General Office

- ☐ Answering the telephone
- ☐ Setting up a meeting
- ☐ Greeting clients
- ☐ Ordering stationery / uniforms
- ☐ Updating insurances
- ☐ General daily procedures
- ☐ _____
- ☐ _____

Sales

- ☐ Sales process
- ☐ Generating new leads
- ☐ Cold-call scripts
- ☐ Follow up processes
- ☐ Understanding targets and KPIs
- ☐ _____
- ☐ _____

Marketing

- ☐ Social media/marketing calendar
- ☐ Scheduling electronic direct marketing (EDMs)

- ☐ Using creative software
- ☐ Copywriting and branding styles
- ☐ _____
- ☐ _____

Financials

- ☐ Entering accounts
- ☐ Paying invoices
- ☐ Generating aged receivables reports
- ☐ Collecting debt
- ☐ Creating an annual budget
- ☐ _____
- ☐ _____

Human Resources

- ☐ Creating clear job descriptions and KPIs
- ☐ Conducting performance reviews
- ☐ Generating policies and procedures
- ☐ Processing annual leave forms
- ☐ First day and onboarding procedures
- ☐ Recruitment system (I'll share this one with you on page 166)
- ☐ _____
- ☐ _____

IT

- [ ] Creating a password policy
- [ ] Updating virus software
- [ ] Troubleshooting equipment
- [ ] Opening attachments
- [ ] Creating a backup policy
- [ ] _____
- [ ] _____

Operations (specific to your industry)

- [ ] _____
- [ ] _____
- [ ] _____
- [ ] _____
- [ ] _____
- [ ] _____
- [ ] _____

TIP FOR QUICK AND EASY SYSTEMS

Outlook templates save you time.

Refer to video in the Interactive Guide on how to create quick and easy email templates.

This has honestly been our best and most time efficient system! Ever!! (it's also the easiest to implement)

Empowering People with Systems: Accountabilities and Reporting

As a business owner, you want things to be done in a certain way. To achieve this, you create systems. You teach your team to use them and then hold them accountable through reporting and measuring. Sounds easy, right?

Well, if only…

Book keeping is an essential task of any business, but is not the best use of a business owner's time. I never really enjoyed this task, but knew the importance of it. So, I held onto it for way too long. Eventually, I hired someone to delegate this task to. It backfired, badly.

For everything that goes wrong in our business we always look for the lessons to improve, and this was one of those pivotal points for us. The problem came down to a lack of systems and mistakenly trusting one person with both accounts receivable and accounts payable. Basically, I did not have the appropriate systems or reporting procedures in place and things unravelled really quickly.

I was scarred after this experience, so for many years I held onto the company accounting tighter than ever. Of course, this was unsustainable. As the business grew, I couldn't keep up with the invoicing and spent my weekends and Christmas holidays catching up on bank reconciliation!

When I eventually systemised it, I was able to outsource the accounts payable invoice entries to an overseas company at a fraction of the cost, and separate the accounts receivable duties in-house. We were now protected and our accounts were accurate for me to analyse the figures monthly. It took me nine long years to give up this process, but wow, I can now sleep at night knowing it is being completed to my high standard.

You might find that once you start implementing systems and measuring performance, the employees who are not delivering (and know it) will suddenly resign. This is usually a good thing for your business.

> **Tell me how I'm measured and I'll show you how I perform."**
> – Anthony Davis

> **What you measure, you manage and what you manage improves."**
> – Anthony Davis

These are two of our favourite quotes. We use them every time we review staff, and it always rings true! It is like going to the gym. If you never measure your results or increase your weights, you can quickly lose motivation.

Systems give team members the freedom to work in a style that suits them and make decisions without being micro-managed. Team members want a leader that will empower them to achieve. Systems create this empowerment by providing staff with a level of ownership over their job.

One of the biggest difficulties large companies have is the roadblocks associated with too many systems, in that only managers or people 'higher up' are able to create or change them. This demotivates team members. Counter this by giving staff the opportunity to have their say regarding processes and procedures, especially those that directly impact the execution of their jobs.

Everyone is (or can be) a leader when given the right environment. By utilising systems, providing staff with clear expectations and regular measures of performance (possibly in the form of KPIs), employees will start improving their performance.

Financial Systems

KNOWING YOUR NUMBER

You know those accounting reports that bore you to tears? Well, they won't be so boring once you learn how to read and understand them. They are crucial tools for making business decisions.

Knowing your number is more than just being aware of your bank balance. Business owners must be able to plan for the future. They must know how to take on healthy debt to expand their business, have sufficient cash flow to ride cyclical waves, and (most importantly) make sure that there is enough cash left over for salaries.

In the early stages of a business, knowing your numbers can be a relatively easy task to keep on top of. However, as a business grows and turn over increases, keeping track of the financials can quickly become daunting. While not everyone has an affinity for numbers, learning how they affect your day to day operations (or finding an advisor to show you) can go a long way in laying those early foundations.

Let's take a look at two important financial indicators: cash flow management and financial statements.

IMPORTANCE OF CASH FLOW MANAGEMENT

Cash flow management is the process of tracking how much money is coming in and going out of a business at any given point in time. Even businesses that appear strong on paper can quickly run into cash flow troubles if their money is not managed well.

The cash flow of a business is tied to its activities or operations. Businesses that have greater outflows than inflows will quickly find that they need to take on debt to service their expenditures. The careful balancing act of cash inflows and outflows is a crucial factor in any business success story. In the early stages of a business, it is not uncommon for businesses to spend more than they earn. Long term, however, businesses should work towards being cash flow positive.

A cash flow positive business will provide the owner with the room and flexibility to make important decisions on future growth. They will be able to pivot where necessary and pay suppliers and staff on time. Most importantly, having positive cash flow provides a business owner with peace of mind by relieving some of the financial stress associated with business management.

SIX TIPS TO HELP WITH BUSINESS CASH FLOW

1. **Keep a regular eye on your accounts**

   Waiting until the end of the month to track cash flow and accounts is often too late. Check how much money is coming in and going out of your business several times each month. This will also give you a better indication of which weeks and months have the greatest inflows and outflows of cash.

2. **Ask for deposits on larger orders**

   Businesses with inventory will quickly come to realise the cash costs associated with holding it. Taking deposits and partial payments on orders can help alleviate some of the monetary burdens of inventory purchasing.

3. **Pay invoices on time but not early**

   Making sure a business has enough cash to pay its obligations is an important part of cash flow management. Pay all invoices when they fall due, rather than early, to make sure you have enough money on hand if something crops up.

4. **Follow up on accounts receivable**

   While it is important to establish business relationships with trade terms, keeping an eye on when invoices are due for payment and sending out friendly reminders can help you get a cash influx when you need it most.

5. **Manage your inventory**

   Making sure that you only hold the inventory you need will free up cash for other important business needs. Unless inventory is sold, it is not going to help with your cash flow needs.

6. **Create a budget**

   Building a detailed monthly (and yearly) budget forecast is a great way to see and understand where money is moving in the business. Highlighting those months that have larger than normal expenses (for example, periods where insurance, tax and super contributions are due) is also helpful.

UNDERSTANDING YOUR FINANCIAL STATEMENTS

Why wait until the end of the financial year to submit your accounts and find out what went right and wrong? By then, it will be too late to make any changes and get back on course! Completing the end of year financials should be treated as a procedural formality only.

Getting to know your financial statements throughout the year will provide an understanding of the current financial health of the business, allow you to forecast for the future, and help you compare business performance month to month. Two reports that will provide you with this important information are the **balance sheet** and the **profit and loss statement**.

BUDGET TIP

The more detailed you are in your budgets, the better management you have over your business.

At Future Fitouts, our annual budget is prepared and broken down with **great** precision. I know our budget and overheads down to the cent at any one time for every account code.

For example, stationery is broken down into about five line items:

1. Paper allowance of [X] quantity per month

2. Courier allowance

3. General stationery allowances

4. Printing charges

5. Paper shredding

(and I've systemised it, so it's quick and easy to update each year)

BALANCE SHEET

The balance sheet is a summary of all your business assets and liabilities at a point in time. It is often called a **statement of financial position** as it provides a snapshot of the value or net worth of your business.

There are two important sections on every balance sheet: **assets** and **liabilities**. The assets section is split into **current assets** and **fixed assets**. Current assets are liquid assets that a business plans to keep for just a short period of time. This can include things like money in a bank account, stock, and trade debtors. Fixed assets are tangible property and may include things like company buildings, equipment, and vehicles. Totalling the current and fixed assets equals the complete value of assets held by a business.

Liabilities are split into **short** and **long term**. Short term liabilities will generally need to be paid within 30 days to one year. Short term loans, trade credits, and bank overdrafts are all examples of short term liabilities. Long term liabilities will generally include any obligations that do not fall due within one year of the balance sheet date.

Use this simple formula to calculate the net worth of your business. Total Assets − Total Liabilities = Owner's Equity (net worth).

Businesses that have a negative net worth can still be cash flow positive. If an owner has taken on debt to start a business, the balance sheet will likely show a negative net worth. This is common and perfectly fine in the short term. Long term, however, high levels of debt can quickly lead to business distress. A business owner should keep an eye on their balance sheet year on year and make positive owner's equity a long-term goal.

PROFIT AND LOSS STATEMENT

Unlike the balance sheet, which provides an indication of the financial position of a business at a point in time, the profit and loss statement (or income statement) shows the profitability of your business over a *period of time* (usually quarterly or annually). It is commonly broken down into two key parts: **revenue** and **expenses**.

The revenue section lists all income derived from primary business activities. Expenses include the cost of goods sold (i.e. the costs associated with selling your goods, including labour and raw materials) and business operation expenses.

When looking at the profit and loss statement there are two key concepts to note.

1. **Gross profit is the profit made after deducting the cost of goods sold from the revenue of selling those products**

2. **Net profit is the profit made after deducting business expenses from the gross profit**

While both are strong dictators of business performance over a period of time, aiming to reduce the costs associated with selling goods will generally lead to a higher gross profit, while reducing business expenses will increase the net profit.

TIP

Profit is always more important than turnover

INVESTING TIME IN YOUR BUSINESS (WORK ON IT, NOT IN IT)

For most entrepreneurs, the start of a new business usually requires significant time and financial investment. While early financial investment can be difficult to come by, expending your own time is an important part of the early stages of business growth. Whether you learn a new skill, complete market research, meet with clients, or network to develop key relationships, the adage that 'time is money' is almost always true. Knowing and understanding the intricacies of how your business operates (and developing trusted relationships with people who can offer expertise to fill in the gaps) is an important step to running a successful business.

Starting a business is not for the faint of heart. There will certainly be ups and downs and road blocks along the way. However, every minute that you invest in your business will feel like a minute well spent. In the future, you will be able to look back on all of your hard work and see some of the defining moments in your business' story.

As a rule of thumb, invest a minimum of three hours per week working on your business rather than in it.

CASE STUDY

Scandinavian Airline System CEO, Jan Carlzon

Author and business leader Jan Carlzon is a global visionary. His greatest feat? Saving Scandinavian Airlines from commercial collapse. How did he do it? By transforming the airline into a first-class client focused and employee empowered company.[2]

During the late 1970s, European airline Scandinavian Airlines was haemorrhaging money. In fact, by 1980, it was estimated the company was losing $17 million per year. On top of this, it was renowned for being late (being ranked 14 of 17 European airlines in terms of punctuality) and was highly centralised. It was obvious that something had to change.

In 1980, Jan Carlzon joined Scandinavian Airlines. By 1981, he was appointed CEO. Within one year of his appointment, Scandinavian Airlines had completely turned around its fate, becoming the most punctual airline in the EU and gaining a huge profit.

Carlzon achieved this by implementing a simple strategy: focus on the client. He considered everything, from how the check in desk was handled, to the way the pilot spoke over the carrier speaker. Every part of the flying process was analysed and altered so that it could better the client experience.

Carlzon then focused his efforts on creating a team of empowered staff. He began decentralising the company by delegating decision making to client facing staff, rather than middle or upper management. He implemented systems so that people 'on the ground' could answer questions and solve problems on the spot without seeking approval from a supervisor. This empowered employees to take responsibility for their roles and clients.

> **Focus on that 1% improvement of 100 things, rather than improving one thing by 100%.**

> 66 *Excellence doesn't mean we have to be 100% better in any one thing: it means we strive to be 1% better in one hundred things."*
> – Jan Carlzon

Recruitment Systems

DOES PAY MATTER?

Of course pay matters!

It is important that you compensate employees what they are worth and show them that they are valued.

However, pay is not the only thing that keeps people in a job.

According to a report by Curtin University[3] based on data from the Household, Income and Labour Dynamics in Australia (HILDA) survey,[4] pay is an integral component of whether or not someone is happy in a job. However, it is not the only factor. Workers in high paying roles are still likely to be dissatisfied if other elements of their job are not favourable.

According to HILDA data, Australian employees who are "'not so satisfied' with work hours tend to earn higher weekly wages, reflecting the trade-off that is made between work and leisure."[5] As well as this, workers who are "dissatisfied with both job security and flexibility will have a higher weekly wage on average than those that are very satisfied with these aspects of their job."[6]

So, if staff aren't just looking for more pay, what is it that they want?

The answer: job satisfaction.

Job satisfaction refers to the sense of fulfilment a person gets from the work that they do. A number of different elements impact whether or not an employee feels satisfied in their job. Remuneration, work hours, flexibility, opportunities for career progression, the type of work, and company ethos are just some of the aspects of a job that contribute to whether an employee is inspired to go the extra mile in their role, or just simply show up and go through the motions.

Generally, people want to be a part of **something they can believe in**. They want to love the work that they do, while doing it for an employer who aligns with their ethics and values.

Job satisfaction is also dependent on the individual: what is satisfying to one person, may not be to another. For example, two colleagues might work in the same role, at the same company. The first finds their job intellectually stimulating, but the second considers it to be boring and lacking in opportunities. This is because everybody has different fulfilment needs.

MASLOW'S HIERARCHY OF NEEDS

In 1943, American psychologist Abraham Maslow developed a model that explained and organised human motivational needs.[7] Coined 'Maslow's hierarchy of needs', the system proposes that to be optimal in health, each of us have five human needs that should be met. These are physiological, safety, belongingness, esteem, and self-actualisation. The five needs are then grouped into three distinct categories: basic needs, psychological needs, and self-fulfilment needs.

Our basic, physiological, and safety needs are at the bottom of the pyramid. 'Physiological' refers to our need for survival (i.e. our need for food, water and rest). 'Safety' relates to our need to feel secure, and can include work, relationship and health security. If these basic needs are not met, then an individual will find it difficult to move up the scale.

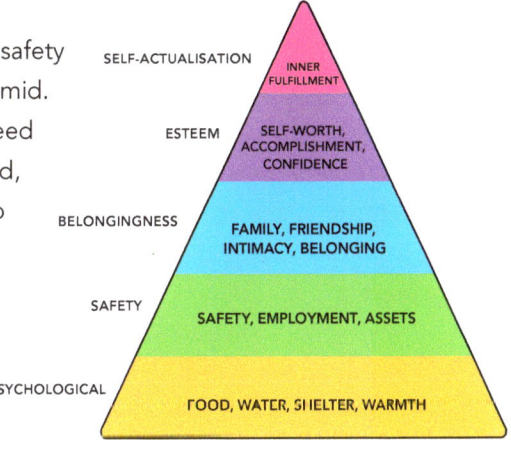

Psychological (belonging) needs are next up the ladder. To fulfil the belonging need, we should feel connected to others and wanted in relationships. Esteem or importance relates to feelings of accomplishment and self-respect.

Self-actualisation sits right at the top of the pyramid. To achieve self actualisation, a person needs to feel that they are achieving their highest potential and are fulfilled in their life.

Translating this model into the workplace is simple and can be applied using the table on the next page.

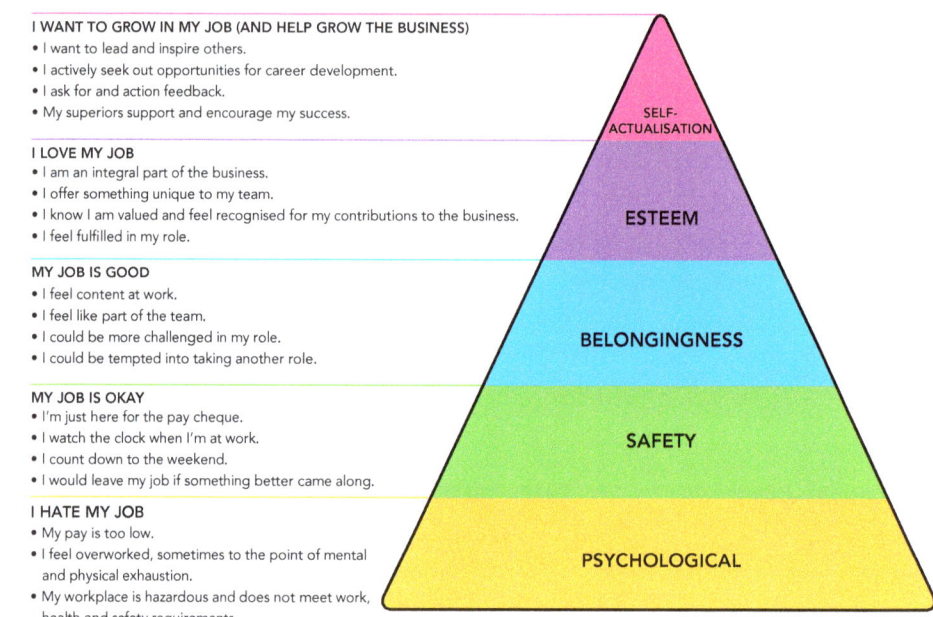

I WANT TO GROW IN MY JOB (AND HELP GROW THE BUSINESS)
- I want to lead and inspire others.
- I actively seek out opportunities for career development.
- I ask for and action feedback.
- My superiors support and encourage my success.

I LOVE MY JOB
- I am an integral part of the business.
- I offer something unique to my team.
- I know I am valued and feel recognised for my contributions to the business.
- I feel fulfilled in my role.

MY JOB IS GOOD
- I feel content at work.
- I feel like part of the team.
- I could be more challenged in my role.
- I could be tempted into taking another role.

MY JOB IS OKAY
- I'm just here for the pay cheque.
- I watch the clock when I'm at work.
- I count down to the weekend.
- I would leave my job if something better came along.

I HATE MY JOB
- My pay is too low.
- I feel overworked, sometimes to the point of mental and physical exhaustion.
- My workplace is hazardous and does not meet work, health and safety requirements.
- I am actively seeking out other employment options.

At Future Fitouts, we want every employee to *at least* feel that their belonging needs are being met at work. Staff should feel valued, respected by their colleagues and connected to the company. We want to instil a sense of trust into every team member so that when they come to work they know, without a shadow of a doubt, that they are needed. To me, this is crucial. If staff do not feel that they belong in your business, then you are at risk of losing them.

So many of us are guilty of giving a team member a pay rise or monetary bonus when often, it is the small gestures that mean so much more. Aaron and I much prefer to give random rewards following specific success, like when a target is reached or a challenging project has been completed. We also don't particularly like the idea of Christmas bonuses, as they can become an expectation for staff, rather than an incentive to go above and beyond. (Remember, staff get paid to come to work. Bonuses are a reward for employees who go the extra mile, not a handout for those who simply show up.)

Refer to Random Acts of Kindness on page 217 for more on this.

What Really Drives Employees at Work?

Believe it or not, it is not money, safety, security, or pressure that drives employees to perform at work. Nor is it the supposedly foundational needs in Maslow's hierarchy. So, what is it?

In a wide-ranging study of employee motivation, Harvard Business School professor Teresa Amabile and psychologist Steven Kramer asked hundreds of employees to maintain a diary chronicling their peaks and valleys in motivation at work[8]. They eventually analysed 12,000 diary entries, and what they discovered was quite surprising. (In fact, Amabile and Kramer talked with 600 managers about what they thought was the single-most important motivator for employees at work. A shocking 95% of them got the answer wrong!)

The most important motivator for employees at work is what Amabile and Kramer call "the power of small wins." Employees are highly productive and driven to do their best work when they feel that they are making progress every day toward a meaningful goal.

Think about how you can motivate your team by creating ways that they can experience feelings of accomplishment. You might try introducing small milestones for bigger projects or setting achievable, yet challenging, targets for tasks.

THE URGENCY TO HIRE

We have learned many lessons over the years (and still learning) and it has been through our greatest challenges that we have discovered the most business changing lessons. During testing times, we have been forced to either change systems or do things differently. The result always ends up positive.

That is not to say that we did not feel disheartened through the rough patches. Quite the opposite. However, running a business is a learning process. Understanding what systems must be in place to prevent unfortunate things happening in the future is something every business owner eventually gets on top of. It all takes time, money and stress.

Interestingly, many of our biggest challenges were in the early days when the office was uninviting and uninspiring. It just goes to show that the environment you create really does impact the success of your business!

After our first failed recruitment process (see page 149 for the story), we started perfecting our systems. Every time someone (or something) didn't work out, I would be straight back to our in-house recruitment system adding more steps, or adjusting and refining the process.

One Sunday afternoon, my sister and brother-in-law (who also have their own business) came around for dinner. We were discussing the backend settings of a shared program that we all used. I went and grabbed my laptop and logged into the settings. To my surprise, I saw that one of our team members had been accessing and manipulating the data. They had been logging into the program at strange times (after hours on weekends, late at night, early in the morning) for no known reason.

After some further investigation, we were able to see what data had been manipulated and discovered that the employee was in the early stages of committing serious fraud. Video surveillance confirmed that they had been trespassing on project sites and the office building. We also found evidence of personal property being taken from us and from project sites. The employee had also planted stolen property at our office and sent emails to subcontractors saying that we had taken their tools and equipment.

I would hate to think how long it would have taken us to pick up on these things, had that one conversation over dinner not taken place! After all, the employee had only been with the company about five weeks! After this particular event, police checks became a mandatory requirement for all new employees. We also locked down all of our IT systems and software programs and developed tighter systems throughout the whole business.

 A bad employee costs you 3-5 times their salary. A good employee is free. A great employee makes a company 5-10 times what you pay them."
– Patrick Bet-David [9]

Identifying the Business Need and Hiring New Staff

As your business grows, so will the need to hire more staff. Hiring can be daunting, stressful and *very* expensive if you get it wrong.

Everyone has a horror story or two (or more) about recruitment, and I want to share ours in the hope that you do not make the same mistakes we did and can move forward faster with a great team. This dreadful experience occurred early on in our business and changed our entire hiring system.

We had hired the first few members of our team during the early years of the business. We didn't really have a hiring process, but what we were doing seemed to be working so we kept it as it was.

As time went on, we were expanding rapidly and eventually needed to hire some extra staff to work on a large contract we had just won. We posted an advertisement on a well known job website looking for staff. A few days later, I received a phone call from a recruiter (the first of many since).

"I have the perfect person for your business," the recruiter said.

Great, I thought. *How easy is this?* I had never dealt with a recruiter before, but assumed the process would be simple.

I asked him to send me the candidate details so that I could review them. Instead, the recruiter launched into a spiel about how the candidate was just what I was looking for – he had years of experience at a great company, could wear multiple hats, and was available immediately. According to the recruiter, I would be crazy *not* to hire him. (Essentially, he gave me the standard sales pitch I hear from *every* recruiter that rings me out of the blue. At least these days I am a little less naïve than I used to be!)

We proceeded to interview with the candidate. It was fine. Nothing really stood out (though, anyone can play perfect during a one hour interview). We were still a little undecided. The salary was a lot more than we wanted to spend, and I had just received the recruiter's contract with their hefty fees for placing this person. That was certainly not in the budget!

Before the candidate had even left the interview, the recruiter was calling me. "How did it go? Can you get the paperwork signed and back to me? This person is in high demand and you will miss out if you don't make a move by 5 pm today. They have other offers!"

My naivety got the better of me. *Far out*, I thought. *This person must be really good, we need them.*

I signed the contract (under obvious pressure) and requested that the recruiter send through references and a police check. We offered the candidate a position with a start date that was almost immediate.

Let's just say that this person's first day wasn't quite what we had expected...

The rest of the staff had left the office very promptly and I was left on my own after a long, hard day. My observation of this person throughout the day made me feel that something wasn't right.

I found myself in tears questioning our decision to hire this person. *What had we done? Had we just made the worst mistake of our lives?* I imagined the type of damage this could do to the business that we had worked so hard for.

It was after 5 pm and my phone rang. It was my husband, Aaron, who had been out all day so we hadn't been able to talk. I answered, trying to hold it together. The first words out of his mouth were, "far out, I think we have made a really bad decision!"

My heart sank. Aaron had just confirmed everything I was thinking. He continued, "I feel like I am an apprentice being yelled at in my own business!" (Aaron is normally a stress free, easy going guy that doesn't let anyone or anything bother him, so the situation *must* have been bad!)

After just *one* day, this person had managed to receive strong negative reactions from multiple people.

- o Our site team had raised a concern with Aaron during the day, stating that if the new employee remained at our company, they would no longer work for us and were ready to walk immediately.

- An office team member came to me and made a complaint in relation to bullying and borderline sexual harassment.

- I was shown no respect during the induction (or all day, for that matter) and had a gut wrenching feeling that we had made a terrible hiring decision.

- Aaron felt he was undermined and questioned on our ethics in the company.

How did we not see this behaviour in the interview? How could we let someone like this into our company? *What had we done?*

I will never forget this long day and the night that followed. At the time, our daughter was about 18 months old and in day care. We called my parents (who are also business owners) for an emergency meeting to discuss what had happened during the day and what we could do about it. (I am very close to my parents, and my dad has a unique way of dealing with people and not putting up with 'idiots'.)

We knew we had to fire this person first thing the next morning. We were terrified! Firing a person is never easy, but having to fire someone that you are already scared of makes it ten times worse! On top of that, this was the first employee we had ever had to fire! However, we knew that the longer they stayed, the more damage they would cause to the business.

Neither of us slept that night. Between a baby waking up for feeds, late night phone calls with our HR consultant, and rehearsing our scripted (very short and straight to the point) speech, we were completely wiped.

Morning rolled around and the sick feeling in my stomach was not going away. We marched straight into the office, called the meeting, and dismissed the employee immediately, not willing to answer questions or offer any justification. The speech that we had spent hours rehearsing was over in under two minutes. However, the next ten seemed to drag on *forever* while we waited for the employee to pack up their belongings and leave the office.

We parted ways, and I wish I could say that was the end of it. Unfortunately, it was just the beginning.

I called the recruiter to tell them what happened and ask whether they had actually carried out the reference checks they said they did.

"Sorry, we ran out of time to do the full reference checks," they said. "But we do have a replacement guarantee and can replace this hire for you."

I was so upset and infuriated. "Really? You think I am going to trust a replacement after this?"

An argument ensued between us and the recruiter and we went back and forth with demands. In a nutshell, we did not think we should be liable for their hefty fee, and we *certainly* did not trust them to try and fill the position again. Could you blame us?

The recruiter didn't agree. The dispute escalated and solicitors got involved. It was then we were advised that, because of the contract conditions, we could not rehire for six months. If we did, we would be liable for the recruiter fee.

A six month hire freeze seemed impossible. We needed someone immediately! Despite my panic, we had no choice but to oblige.

About one month later, I received a phone call from a debt collection agency demanding payment for the recruiter's fees. They told me that a bad credit rating had been registered on our company name.

I could not believe it. We had had a perfect credit rating that (through no fault of our own) was now being ruined!

Thankfully, I was able to reason with the debt collector. He couldn't believe that the recruiter was still chasing us for the money when the employee was only with us for one day! We ended up paying a small sum to settle the matter and the credit red flag check was removed.

The course of these events was an absolute game changer for our business. We learned the best possible lessons we could, and took away only the positives. From this, we developed our own in-house 12 step robust recruitment system. Our system does not need recruiters, but if we do decide to work with them, they work on our terms.

On a side (slightly funny) note: about four years later, a completely different recruiter at a different company called us out of the blue and put the same person forward to us again! I couldn't help but laugh.

IDENTIFYING THE BUSINESS NEED AND HIRING NEW STAFF

The bottom line is, if your current recruitment system is not working for you or the culture you are creating, change it. You may want to implement some of the strategies we have put in place (outlined below), or you can come up with your own. It is up to you. Have fun with it and remember that your hiring process can be as selective as you choose.

If you do decide to use recruiters, do yourself a favour and read the fine print. Do your research *before* you get involved.

RECRUITMENT IS LIKE A PIZZA (ON A FIRST DATE)!

In Part Five, I will share with you our 12 step secret recruitment system that has been refined over the years. This system has saved us tens of thousands of dollars in recruitment fees and has helped us attract the best and most culturally fit people for our team. It has been tested throughout every single one of our hires (and fires). Every time a team member leaves, we revisit this system and reflect upon whether there is anything that should be changed or improved.

I have asked countless interview candidates what they thought of our recruitment process, and the feedback has always been very positive. I have heard everything from, "wow, I thought I was just coming in for a standard job interview" and "I've never seen anything so detailed and accurate," to, "I can see why this process works and reflects the culture in your company." One candidate even said, "I don't think this is the right place for me." All of these were great answers. This question alone forms part of our system.

If recruitment is like a pizza, then the size of each slice is determined by the position requirements. Some requirements have a greater emphasis than others. Each slice (no matter how narrow or wide) represents a component to make up the 'perfect' candidate and ultimately both people proceeding with the date (aka. signing the employment contract).

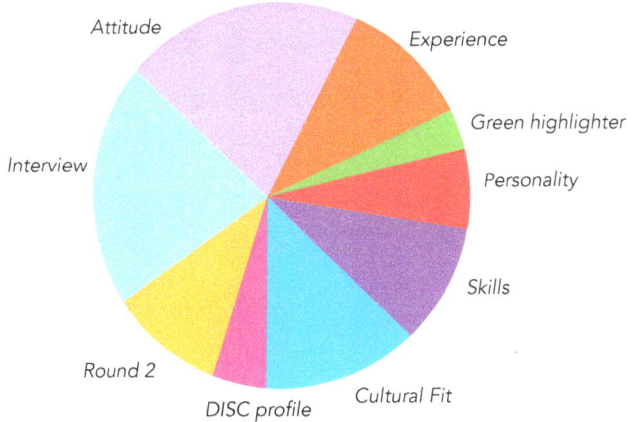

The first interview is like a first date, both parties are asking a lot of questions and determining if they wish to proceed and meet again. However, throw a pizza in the mix and the aim of recruitment is to get the most number of slices to complete the pizza (or come close to making a full pizza as possible – unicorn employees are rare). (This will make a lot more sense if you turn to page 166 and would like to jump straight to our 12 step recruitment system.)

Mistakes That Business Owners Make During Hiring

Trust me, we have made all of them!

1. The need to hire yesterday

Business owners get so caught up in the urgency to fill a role, that they can make the common mistake of 'selective hearing' during interviews. Often, the interviewer will focus only on the candidate's 'good points', choosing to ignore their limitations or insufficient qualifications. Often, the owner will justify why the candidate is the right fit for the position and company.

The solution: Include one or two external panel members on your interview panel. These should be people that can provide you with varying, non-biased perspectives of the candidate. Supplementary panel members might see and hear things differently to you, and will be able to ask questions that you have not thought of.

2. Doing all the talking

It is true that the candidate is there to learn more about your business. However, with so much online, the (good) candidates will have already done their research by stalking your socials, asking others in the industry about you, and filtering through your website and online reviews. Chances are they are only at the interview stage because they liked what they saw. Try not to waste time during the interview talking about your company. Instead, use your time wisely by asking questions and *really listening* to the candidate.

The other common mistake that interviewers make is in their questioning. Either the interviewer asks a great question, but also gives the answer away, *or* they ask a closed question, which means the candidate can only provide a yes or no response. For example, rather than asking, "Have you worked with a difficult client before?" say, "Provide me with two examples of working with a difficult client, why were they difficult, and how you handled it." Remember, you want the candidate to do most of the talking throughout the interview.

The solution: Frame the same question multiple ways and ask questions that require answers with examples.

3. **Only having one interview**

   Again, the urgency to hire often limits employers to scheduling just one interview with each candidate. But think about it – an interview lasts between 30 minutes to an hour. During that time, the candidate is madly 'selling' themselves while the owner is trying to fill a hole in their company as soon as possible (using as little resources as possible). There really is not enough time for either party to form a relationship.

   The solution: Schedule more than one interview, even if you think you have found the right person after the first meeting. When we hire, we always schedule two formal interviews per candidate, each with a different panel member. On occasion, we request a third catch up interview in a more social setting with the rest of the team.

   The first interview is generally just finding out about the person's career history and experience. If they are shortlisted for the second interview, the candidate is much more relaxed and open. It is at this stage that we learn more about them and can gauge who it is that will be 'showing up for work' every day. Having more than one interview also gives the candidate a chance to digest the information from the first interview and come back with interesting questions.

4. **Hiring for attitude (instead of for skill)**

   This is an interesting (and debatable) concept. Hiring for skill is generally a good idea when you are first starting out and growing a team, or have lower budgets to work with. You can get your business off the ground more quickly by hiring talented people, rather than hiring someone at a 'lower level'. (Eventually, your business will reach a point where skill and attitude are equally as important!)

   Many business owners make the mistake of hiring just for attitude so that they can pay 'start up' salaries. Remember, if you need to train someone, it will cost you in time which is ultimately money. As you grow, you will be able to afford to pay more for your staff. You eventually want to be surrounded by a team that are more experienced and knowledgeable than you, which often comes at a higher price.

   The solution: Don't make the mistake of hiring someone just because they are cheaper than someone with more experience. Attitude and cultural fit will always be important, however should not overshadow the skills required to fulfil position.

5. **Hiring someone like you**

   You have interviewed someone who is just like you. You have similar personalities, you get along like a house on fire, and they somehow just *get it*. You're thinking, *this is great! What a perfect match for my company!*

   The problem with this is that your personality profile will not suit every role. By hiring multiple people just like 'you', you endanger finding someone who is the best fit for your company's requirements. (I explain this in greater detail in the Extended DiSC® section on page 179)

   The solution: All great businesses require a combination of personality types and different behavioural styles to succeed. Identify what the perfect person for the role would look like, and hire based on that (rather than simply hiring someone that you think you would get along with). Finding the right people for each role is essential if your company is going to perform at its best. Hire people smarter than you.

6. Ignoring those gut feelings

Have you ever had that little niggling feeling that something doesn't sit right? Trust it! Don't make the mistake of ignoring how you feel just to make something work. In business (and in life) your gut feeling is often right. Learn to trust and believe in it.

The solution: If you aren't great at trusting your own instincts, ask others for their opinions or impressions. Females, in particular, tend to have stronger intuition and judgement.

Feeling overwhelmed? I get it. There is *a lot* to think about. However, once you have spent the time creating your hiring systems, it will be very easy to adapt them as you grow and new roles are created. Having a solid hiring process in place will save you a lot of heartache and help your business attract world class talent.

THE TIMING AND COST OF GETTING IT WRONG!

Hiring the right person can be a lengthy process. A company needs to find someone that not only possesses the right technical skills for the role, but has the right personality to fit into the workplace culture. To ensure that the most suitable person is hired, a great deal of time and resources are dedicated to figuring out which candidate is the best fit. An additional salary is just one aspect of bringing in a new team member. It is the cost of hiring and onboarding a new employee that can quickly add up.

Let's take a deeper look at the hidden costs of hiring a new employee.

THE COST OF RECRUITING

Occasionally, you might get lucky and the perfect candidate applies before you have even started the recruitment process. Most of the time, however, a lot of money and resources need to be expended to find the right person. Setting up the advertisement (or using a recruiter), conducting interviews, and processing administrative paperwork all cost your company resources. If you multiply the average hourly wage (roughly $36 according to the Australian Bureau of Statistics' August 2020 reference period) with the 20 (but likely more) hours of combined employee efforts dedicated to processing candidates, the cost of employing someone new can quickly skyrocket.

Think about how long the following basic recruitment tasks would take, and how much they would cost:

1. Writing a job description

2. Sourcing a recruitment agency or posting an advertisement to job boards

3. Reviewing applications

4. Corresponding with applicants

5. Interviewing applicants

6. Conducting background and reference checks

THE COST OF ONBOARDING A NEW EMPLOYEE

The administrative process of hiring a new employee, or onboarding, can take quite a lot of time. Onboarding involves adding the employee to systems and processes, filling out administrative papers and contracts, and introducing them to clients and colleagues. These are just a few things to factor into the cost of onboarding a new employee. Onboarding costs will vary depending on the size of the organisation and level of role difficulty.

THE COST OF TRAINING A NEW EMPLOYEE

You will need to dedicate time to training as it is unlikely that a new employee will understand how to use your software, systems or processes. This usually results in both the trainer and the new employee allocating non billable hours to training. If the job requires perpetual learning (such as any digital media based role), training costs should be factored in yearly.

THE COST OF EQUIPMENT
A new employee will require a desk, chair, assets (a computer, telephone or mobile phone plan, and motor vehicle), and subscriptions to software programs and communication systems. All up, this can easily add up to thousands of dollars or more. If a new hire has resulted in the need for an upsized office space, increased rental costs should also be factored into the cost of employment.

THE COST OF BENEFITS
The cost of hiring should factor in benefits such as sick pay, annual leave, tax, and superannuation. A good accountant or book keeper should be able to give you a breakdown of these costs and actual billable hours that the employee can generate.

COST OF A BAD HIRE
There are far deeper consequences than just losing a salary when making a bad hire. An employee who is not pulling their weight or getting along with colleagues can have a serious impact on team morale. Other colleagues may have to pick up the slack, which can result in lowered productivity and rising resentment. If the bad hire is in a managerial position, this can also cause a ripple effect of mass quitting from disgruntled employees. In addition to money spent on wages, a bad hire can end up costing your company tens of thousands of dollars.

TIPS TO MAKE IT EASIER (HAVING SYSTEMS!)
ADVERTISE *BEFORE* YOU REQUIRE THE ROLE
Why on earth would you advertise for positions before you need them, or before the role exists? Simple. When you need a position filled, the 'perfect' candidate may not be looking. The top performers in any industry are always in high demand, so these candidates don't always rely on job searching websites for employment.

You don't need to pay to run continuous advertisements for specific roles, but having a general advertisement permanently up on your website is a great way that you can capture talent year round. Plus pair this with your online presence and reputation in the industry, talent will start coming to you.

We keep the below ad fixed to our careers page on our website. This enable us to collect our own database of candidates, screening them as they apply. We choose to reach out to those candidates who are the best fit.

If and when the right roles become available, we have already skipped the time consuming advertising process. Further, if the candidate already knows about our company, what we stand for, and have meet the team, we will be much closer to making them an offer. We have hired a number of roles using this process.

HEADHUNTING

I am personally not a fan of head hunting, and many of our staff are *constantly* head hunted for other roles. (It is nice to know that they choose to tell us about it and most politely decline the offer, which speaks volumes for the culture we have created!)

There are many people who inadvertently advertise your company for you; think clients, suppliers, consultants, and in some cases recruiters. Many of our current staff initially heard about our company through word of mouth.

WORKING WITH RECRUITERS

As discussed earlier in this book, I am not the biggest fan of working with recruiters. However, there is always an exception to any rule.

If you enjoy engaging recruiters and it works for you, keep using this platform. However, I do suggest that you implement a few of the below tips to minimise any potential risk and ensure a greater success rate.

1. Limit yourself to working with one or two recruiters at any one time

Make sure that you have personally met them, explained the culture to them, and immersed them into your business. When I first started working with the (very few) recruiters we do use, I spent up to half a day with each of them. They joined in on the morning exercise with the team, observed our goal board, and absorbed our values, mission and vision. Because of this, I know that they only send me candidates that have been screened and vetted to culturally fit in our business, rather than just any applicant that crosses their desks.

2. **Good recruiters work for you all year round, not just when you need a role filled!**

   A good recruiter should know the industry inside and out. They will know who is hiring, firing, changing roles or open to looking for opportunities. Want to understand the market and what your competitors are doing? Spend some time with a recruiter!

3. **Negotiate on your terms**

   At a minimum, we ask for a replacement period of 12 months (three months is generally standard). I also negotiate the recruiter's fees.

   Even if recruiters are involved, we will still use our recruitment system concurrently and do a lot of the work ourselves. We have a very open and understanding relationship with our recruiters and they respect us to use our own system in conjunction with theirs. Sometimes, we request that our process is followed by them.

   We are also conscious of which other companies they represent. We have no issue with recruiters representing competitors. Every company is different and has their own unique qualities. When a recruiter knows your company and culture, it won't matter if they are working for the competition. It is just nice to know who else in your industry that they work for.

Lauren is sharing more in her INTERACTIVE book.

See exclusive videos, audios and photos.

DOWNLOAD it now at deanpublishing.com/futureofbusiness

COME JOIN OUR TEAM!

Your FUTURE with FUTURE FITOUTS!

Be part of a company that is "Changing the World by Transforming Spaces!" **[the vision]**

For the right person, working at Future Fitouts will be challenging, rewarding, fast paced, exciting, and of course, inspiring! Our entire team "delivers leading edge commercial fitouts that empower businesses to achieve by transforming work spaces into inspiring environments." **[the mission]**

We are always looking for the right people **[the values]** to join our team, because the right person isn't always available when we are hiring. We are a growing company with a pipeline of work and exciting opportunities! This means that there could be an awesome opportunity waiting just for you…

Continue reading to find out more!

Are you looking for a fast paced, challenging, rewarding and exciting environment?

How would it feel to deliver inspiring commercial fitouts that empower other businesses to achieve great things?

Do you want to join a team where you will gain so much more than 'just a job' and become part of a company that is Changing the World by Transforming Spaces, one space at a time?

You are…

- A life-long learner who is open to new ideas and embraces change and personal growth
- Confident in your abilities to multi-task, plan and organise
- An exceptional communicator (both written and oral)
- Driven by consistent results/KPI's and can deliver projects on time and on budget
- A natural at problem solving, critical thinking and are 'solution' minded
- A glass half full person with a positive and enthusiastic vibe
- Genuine, honest and have a willingness to help the team around you
- Committed to the 'Future Fitouts Way', including our vision, mission and values
- Highly experienced in using Microsoft Word, Excel, and Outlook

What's in it for you?

- Surrounded by a great team that will push you to become better each day
- Vibrant, fun and inspiring work environment
- Attractive packages – negotiable depending on experience
- ……………………………………………………………………………………
……………………………………………………………………………………
……………………………………………………………………………………
……………………………………………………………………………………

PART FIVE

ATTRACT AND RETAIN TALENT

(Positive attracts positive!)

… PART FIVE: ATTRACT AND RETAIN TALENT

Our Secret Recruitment System (12 Step Process)

THE HIRING PROCESS: WHAT DO I DO NOW?

1. Planning the role
2. Advertising
3. Reviewing the applications (Round One)
4. Deal Breaker Round Two (Questionnaire)
5. Random phone call
6. DiSC profile
7. First interview
8. Reference checks
9. Second interview
10. Police check and health questionnaire
11. Offer (and celebrate)
12. Notify unsuccessful candidates

STEP ONE
PLANNING THE ROLE

The first and perhaps most critical step!

Plan the role BEFORE you advertise. You need to have clarity on exactly what the position looks like, the skill set required, the responsibilities, the KPIs, and the justification on why the business needs it. If you are not clear on this as soon as you start the advertising process, you will end up hiring someone just because you 'like them' and not necessarily because they meet the role requirements. This person will ultimately become part of your business family, so you want to get it right.

There are two components to this.

Part A: Job Position Analysis
Identify why the business requires the position and what it looks like.

Consider things like who the position reports to (and vice versa), what is the employment type of the position (i.e. full time, part time, or casual), the outcomes and accountabilities of the position and the tasks to be performed by the position.

Then think about who the ideal candidate would be for that role. You will need to outline specific criteria that the candidate will need to possess to be successful in the position, for example qualifications, skills, and experience. What would their DiSC® profile be and which other companies would they have worked for? Do you have any deal breakers when it comes to hiring?

An example of our Job Position Analysis can be found in the interactive book.

Part B: Create the Position Description

Many employees have either never received a position description, or if they have, it doesn't reflect their actual duties and is a document that is just signed and shelved. At Future Fitouts, the position descriptions we provide are extremely detailed and form part of our onboarding and training plan for the initial three to six months of hire. The documents include references to our systems for each task and the corresponding KPIs. The position descriptions also form part of our review process. (They are not provided at the recruitment stage due to their voluminous size and would probably scare candidates off. Also, we don't want elements of our intellectual property to end up in our competitors' hands.)

An example of our Job Position Description can be found in the Interactive Book.

STEP TWO
ADVERTISING

Once you are clear on the role, it's time to start advertising.

The advertisement needs to be written in a way that will attract the right type of people to your business. The key components of any written advertisement are numbered below.

1. **Overview of the position**

2. **Key outcomes, duties and responsibilities**

3. **List of skills and experience**

4. Company information

5. Outline of perks and benefits

6. What your company offers to attract world class talent (benefits and perks)

7. Next steps

I have set out our game changing template to create the perfect job listing. (What I am giving you now is our intellectual property and a key part of our recruitment system!)

ADVERTISEMENT WORDING	WHAT WE ARE LOOKING FOR
Please send a one page cover letter summarising your [specific experience relevant to the role*]. *Ask specific questions or request detailed information that the candidate should address in their cover letter. This can include examples of their education and programs, experience in the industry and with clients, achievements and awards.	Can the candidate follow instructions? Is the cover letter generic? Did they respond to the questions? Is the cover letter addressed correctly?
Please also send your CV to email@addresshere.com.au with "Company Name – Career Opportunity – [Role Title]" in the subject field.	Please also send your CV to email@addresshere.com.au with "Company Name – Career Opportunity – [Role Title]" in the subject field.
Applications will close at [time and date].	Setting a deadline creates a sense of urgency and will test whether the candidate can deliver on time. Setting a closing deadline will also give you a date that you can review the applications in bulk. This will save you time.

Due to the high volume of applications, only suitable candidates will be notified to progress to the next stage. If successful, you will be asked to complete a DiSC® Profile, Health Questionnaire and Police Check.	This saves you time, as you will only be responding to suitable candidates. This notifies candidates that these things will be requested. If someone does have a police record, the likelihood of them applying will be reduced.
Only people with the right to work in Australia may apply for this position.	Suggests that legal and compliance rights to work will be tested.
Respectfully, please no recruiters.	Limits calls from recruiters, which can be very distracting. We also advise our key recruiters when we are advertising.

STEP THREE
REVIEWING THE APPLICATIONS (ROUND ONE)

You have successfully advertised the position and it is now time to review the applications. Because you have already completed step one, you will be clear on exactly what you want. This will accelerate the hiring process.

We skim each application at the outset and make a quick assessment of each candidate by considering:

1. Whether they have followed the advertisement steps and responded appropriately

2. Whether there are any obvious spelling or grammatical errors in their submissions

3. Whether they have worked at similar companies or have the experience required

We make a shortlist by scoring the top applicants and then collate the information on a spreadsheet. This lets us review all of the candidates in the one place.

STEP FOUR
DEAL BREAKER – ROUND TWO (QUESTIONNAIRE)

This is by far my **favourite** (and probably the most effective) step! We can usually pick our candidate from the questionnaire alone prior to any interview.

Anyone can write a great resume, or pay someone else to do it. It is even possible to upload a curriculum vitae (CV) online and have it turned around in a few hours to look visually appealing, spell checked and presentable.

However, it is near impossible to fake the questionnaire. This carefully constructed survey also provides insight into who the candidate is as a person. You will be able to get a better idea of who it is that you are *actually* employing, rather than the person who is trying to impress by relying solely on the CV.

This round is great as it gives candidates the opportunity to express themselves through written communication prior to interview. This is particularly useful for candidates who find interviews confronting and ensures that they can put their best foot forward. Applicants will also become a little more accustomed to our business and can deselect themselves if they feel they do not fit.

The questionnaire is around three pages long and takes less than 30 minutes to complete. It is comprised of short answer, multiple choice, and problem solving questions that relate to the role. We have purposely designed the document to include different fonts, inconsistent formatting, spelling mistakes, and grammatical errors. The number of errors placed in the document depends on the role and the importance of attention to detail. For example, our administrator roles are required to have a high attention to detail, so their questionnaires will contain 13 mistakes. Project Managers are hired on their ability to deliver projects, so a spelling mistake here or there is not a deal breaker. Estimators need to be familiar with Microsoft Excel, so a basic test is embedded into their document. You can really do anything in this round that tests the candidate.

How does it work?
You've briefly reviewed the candidate's CV and cover letter and deem them

suitable to progress to the next stage. A candidate will receive a template email (to save time) notifying them they have made it to round two. The email will include specific instructions around formatting, response time, and how they are required to respond. This will again test whether the applicant can follow instructions. We are a systemised company, so I need to be confident that my team can follow processes (as well as think outside the box to improve old ones and create new ones).

ROUND TWO EMAIL TEMPLATE	WHAT WE ARE LOOKING FOR
Hi **[Candidate Name]** Thank you for your interest in the **[Title]** position at **[Company Name]**. Your application has been received and reviewed by Management who would like to consider you for round two of the recruitment process. If you are interested in proceeding, please review the **attached** documents and complete the questionnaire. Your responses will assist us in determining your progression to the next round. Make sure that your answers are formatted to 11 point Calibri, left justified. Please complete and return the questionnaire within two business days to ensure a timely process of your application. Email your responses to email@specificaddress.com.au with 'Round Two – Job Title' in the subject line. We have also **attached** a copy of our vision, mission and values for your information. Thank you again for your interest in this position.	We are assessing whether the applicant can work within set timeframes. I have heard numerous excuses why candidates cannot return the questionnaire within two days. If an excuse is legitimate, I allow an extension. If the applicant is showing signs of laziness, or they feel that they are above the requirements of the questionnaire and request an interview only, then we do not proceed with the application. Every single member in our company has followed this exact process.

I have included a snapshot of the round two document below.

ROUND TWO DOCUMENT (EXAMPLE)	WHAT WE ARE LOOKING FOR
PART A: SHORT ANSWER QUESTIONS	
<ul><li>What interests you most about this position?</li><li>How do our vision, mission and values resonate with you?</li><li>What is something in your life that you are proud to have achieved?</li><li>Provide an example of something you have done (in your current or immediate past position) to make a difference.</li><li>How would your best friend describe you?</li><li>Detail any experience you have with ordering materials in the office fitout industry, with reference to specific suppliers and products that you have used.</li><li>Imagine that you have no budget left in the project you are working on. How do you 'wow' the client?</li><li>Name three things that you are grateful for today.</li><li>Name the top three books you have read or movies you have seen. Why have you chosen these?</li><li>How do you prepare for a successful project handover?</li></ul>	Some questions are designed to give us personal insight into the candidate, such as their family life and hobbies outside of work. For example, one question asks what the candidate is grateful for (with gratitude being one of our core values). We usually find out more about the applicant, such as whether they are married or if they have children at this stage. The top three books or movies question serves as a talking point in the interview (if they get to that stage) and provides insight into how the candidate spends their time. Do they enjoy documentaries, crime novels, cartoons, or self development texts?

PART A: SHORT ANSWER QUESTIONS (CONTINUED)

- How do you keep organised and manage projects concurrently?
- Please identify your desired salary range for this position, and if successful, when you would be available to start.

Some questions will be consistent for every role, whereas others are adapted to fit the position.

These short answer questions are designed to see how the candidate relates to our values and how they will culturally fit into the company.

PART B: MULTIPLE CHOICE

1. **There are two shirts with different printing, which one do you choose?**
   (a) No Pain, No Gain
   (b) Life was meant to be easy

   These questions have a bit more psychology behind them.

   The t shirt question determines whether the candidate is someone who makes things happen, or prefers to go with the flow.

2. **I do my tax on time because:**
   (a) I like to get a refund.
   (b) I am less stressed when it is done.

   The tax refund question relates to their drive. Option (a) "I like to get a refund" is the preferred answer.

IMPORTANT NOTE

Include different fonts, inconsistent formatting, spelling mistakes, and grammatical errors throughout the document to test each candidate's attention to detail.

PART B: MULTIPLE CHOICE (CONTINUED)	
3. **Please rate the following from one to three, with one being the easiest.** When I have a project to do, I find it easier to: _Start it _Change it _Finish it	Question three is interesting. Depending on the role, some order preferences are better than others. In general terms, people are either starters or finishers. There is no right or wrong answer, but understanding what types of people you have in your team will assist you when distributing projects. Starters will be better at kicking off a project, but may become sidetracked and want to start new tasks before old ones are completed. Pairing a starter and a finisher together will give you the perfect balance.
4. **Imagine that you love cake. You and your friends have all had one piece of cake and there is only one slice left. You are still hungry. Do you:** (a) Take the last piece? (b) Leave it for someone else?	Question four is testing teamwork and honesty. We have had some candidates offer creative responses to this, showing that they can think outside the box.
5. **When you make appointments, you regularly arrive:** (a) Before time. (b) On time. (c) A few minutes late.	Question five is designed to find out how the applicant manages their time and whether they have answered honestly. If they selected answer (a) but are late to the interview, we ask the question again. If they have picked (c), we know that they have given an honest answer.

PART B: MULTIPLE CHOICE (CONTINUED)

**And just for fun, not a requirement for the position **

6. **How much do you love (or hate) assembling Ikea furniture? (and why?)**
    (a) Hate it! I'm never going to Ikea again!
    (b) Neutral, I'll do it if I have to.
    (c) Love it! I will happily do it in my spare time.

Finally, the last question tests a level of patience and attention to detail, which helps paint a small picture for the DiSC® profile.

PART C: SCENARIO

The following scenario occurs at work*. Please detail your response (no more than half a page).

*Create a scenario that is specific to the role and company. Base it on a real life example if you can. For example, is your receptionist required to answer phone calls, greet guests and sign for deliveries all at the same time? Ask the candidate how they would approach this type of multi-tasking.

You could include a scenario that is based on a specific challenge that your team has come up against. Ask the applicant how they would tackle the problem.

A candidate's response will provide an indication of how they think and the logical process they go through to solve a problem. If you have used an industry specific scenario, you will be able to determine whether their skillset and ability is fit for the role.

We word these scenarios so that we can receive a number of key answers. Some candidates 'get it' and provide a detailed response, while others write a very short and simple answer that ignores the question.

Success rate

Surprisingly, a number of potential candidates never respond to this round. This is perfect for us, as it means that there are less applications to review because they have deselected themselves for whatever reason.

We have been criticised by outsiders in the past (namely recruiters) that round two is too time consuming and candidates won't want to go through all the steps. My belief is that someone who is looking for work or really wants to work for your company will follow the process. Every single member in our team has jumped through these hoops to work for us and have told me how much they appreciated the entire process. If an applicant is not prepared to complete a quick questionnaire, they are probably not the right fit for our business.

EXTRA TIP

We also complete a social media check on the candidate during this stage. (Be honest, who doesn't do a little social media stalk!)

Reviewing responses

Once the responses to round two start coming through, you will notice who has put thought and effort into their application, and begin to see who your standout candidates are. You will gain some understanding of who each applicant is as a person, some of their hobbies, interests, family life, and how they resonate with your visions of the company. Their true personality will start to show.

We do not rely solely on this step (or any step for that matter) to make our decision. The idea behind the pizza theory is to work out the size and importance of each slice and fill in as much of the pizza as possible to find the perfect candidate.

After we have reviewed the questionnaires, we add comments and scoring to our spreadsheet. We base the scores on a set of weighted criteria. This includes whether the responses were submitted on time, if the candidate used correct grammar, spelling, and formatting, and the level of quality provided in the answers. Some responses receive a higher weighting than others.

You should aim to narrow the pool down to no more than six applicants after this round. These are the people who progress to the next stage: Step Five.

STEP FIVE
RANDOM PHONE CALL

We like to test each applicant's phone manner by catching them off guard. We give them a quick ring, introducing where we are calling from and asking whether it is a suitable time to talk. (They might be sitting in an open plan office in their current role and can't chat or be overly friendly.) We keep the conversation very high level and don't go into detail. The purpose of the call is just to acknowledge that we have received their completed questionnaire.

1. **If their phone manner is professional and engaging, we explain that the next step is for us to send a DiSC® behavioural profile to be completed and returned. We let them know that we may invite them for an interview following these results.**

2. **If their phone manner is not ideal or border line rude (particularly if the role is client facing) we politely explain that we are still assessing applications and will be in touch if we need anything further.**

What we are looking for during this call

- How do they answer the phone?
- What is their phone manner like?
- If the call goes to voicemail, is the message appropriate?
- Do they call back (if they have missed the call or were unable to talk)?
- Are they engaging?
- Are they *really* interested in the position, or have they just applied for 'another job'?

STEP SIX
DISC® PROFILE

This is where things start to get exciting!

Before proceeding to a face-to-face interview, we request that each applicant complete a DiSC® profile assessment.

It's the little things!

The DiSC profile is a great way to see if a candidate is a good fit for the role and culture of a company, and can give valuable insight into an applicant's personality and behaviour. The assessment assists owners or direct managers in knowing the type of person that is being employed and the best way to communicate and interact with them.

What is DISC®?

Based on Dr William Marston's findings (first published in his 1928 book, *Emotions of Normal People*),[1] DiSC is one of the leading behavioural assessment tools. It is used around the world by over one million people every year to improve productivity, communication and teamwork in the workplace.[2]

The DiSC profiling system identifies and assesses how different personalities will naturally behave in certain situations and under pressure. When a candidate completes a DiSC assessment, they are measured against four personality profiles: dominant, inspiring, supportive and cautious (or conscientious).[3] A report is then formulated that outlines which mixture of profiles the candidate possesses. (Generally, every person will be a combination of the styles. A DiSC score delineates which profiles someone leans toward more.) This can assist leaders when hiring, as a DiSC report will clearly show each candidate's natural strengths and traits, and thus, what role they would be most suited to.

Dominance

Person places emphasis on accomplishing results, the bottom line and confidence.

Behaviours

- Sees the big picture
- Can be blunt
- Accepts challenges
- Gets straight to the point

Influence

Person places emphasis on influencing or persuading others, openness and relationships.

Behaviours

- Shows enthusiasm
- Is optimistic
- Likes to collaborate
- Dislikes being ignored

Conscientiousness

Person places emphasis on quality and accuracy, expertise and competency.

Behaviours

- Enjoys independence
- Objective reasoning
- Wants the details
- Fears being wrong

Steadiness

Person places emphasis on cooperation, sincerity and dependability.

Behaviours

- Doesn't like to be rushed
- Calm manner
- Calm approach
- Supportive actions

Interpreting the letters (and introducing the animals)

When explaining DiSC® profiling to job applicants, there are often many "uh huh!" moments. People cannot believe how accurate their results are! Often, candidates will tell us that their profile sounds exactly like them.

I usually explain the profile with a simple drawing that summarises each trait and how they interact with one another. I then relate these behaviours to an animal.

Bull

Speeds up when under pressure and appears more extraverted.

Dominating, hard values, fast, gets it done, no time for niceties, high level detail.

Biggest fear: losing control, not being in charge.

Peacock

People oriented.

Social, popular, friendly, positive, animated talker. Think of a peacock walking into a room with their feathers on display for everyone to see.

Biggest fear: being left out.

Owl

Likes to perfect the job at hand.

Think of an owl's two eyes: perfectionist, analytical, precise, accurate.

Biggest fear: not being given correct information, submitting work that is not accurate.

Sheep

Slows down when under pressure. Appears more introverted and reserved.

The support that hold the team together. Patient, calm, good listener, steady.

Biggest fear: not having enough time to complete a task, dealing with too many changes.

Another very common method of identifying DiSC traits is using the 'Elevator Test'.

Assume there are four people waiting for an elevator to arrive. The first person (D type) is rushing towards the door, pressing the button continually to speed it up. Another person is waiting to greet everyone who is exiting the lift (I type). The third person stands back waiting for the others to get in and out and gently tucks themselves towards the back of the elevator so as not to disturb others (S type). The final person looks up at the compliance plate to calculate the capacity of the elevator and determine if the right number of people are inside (O type).

Head to the Interactive Book for a video on this!

Workplace DiSC®

DiSC is the most popular assessment tool for team building, employee communication, conflict management, motivation, productivity and career development. DiSC is about building relationships around the office. It provides users with valuable insights into the behaviours and motivations of staff and can be used to create strong and positive teams.

Once you understand the basics of DiSC, you can start using it to your advantage. I have completed numerous courses on DiSC and have finished my training to become an accredited DiSC assessor. However, I am by no means an expert and sometimes rely on other trained providers to interpret the graphs for me.

The information included in this book has been explained at very high level as the process can be quite in depth. Understanding the shape of the lines, comparing profiles (natural state and environment), and numerous other considerations go into fully understanding and interpreting the profile results. There are many online tools available that can provide you with a DiSC profile and clearly explain the results of the graphs (both free or a for small fee). Making this investment at the recruitment stage may save you thousands in a wrong hire.

If you are not comfortable with the online self-assessment tools, you can engage a consultant to run sessions with you and explain the power of this tool and assist in interpreting the data. Make sure that whatever provider you use is trained and is available to explain the results, debrief candidates, and answer your questions.

Hiring: right people, right roles

Once you have someone's DiSC® results, you need to ensure they are suited for the role/tasks you need them to carry out. Anybody can perform tasks in areas that they aren't necessarily 'profiled' for. But, if it's not their natural style, they will use **more energy completing the tasks, which is not sustainable** long term. Using DiSC® will ensure that you are putting the right people in the right roles.

When you are recruiting for a role, you must first consider the preferred combination of the DiSC profile, and *then* find candidates who match it. For example, if you are hiring an accounts clerk and need someone with a high level of attention to detail and ability to follow systems, the ideal profile would be 'CS' or 'SC' – someone who naturally enjoys detail, is analytical, can follow instructions and enjoys routine. If you hired a D profile for this role by mistake, it could be a disaster waiting to happen. Not only is it unnatural for a D profile to focus on detail (this would require more energy and result in higher level of stress), but they would get bored very easily following routine work. If you were hiring for sales, you would need someone who could naturally engage with people. Therefore, looking for a profile with 'I' in it would be ideal. (But be careful in this example as the biggest fear for an 'I' is rejection, so a sales role requiring cold-calling wouldn't be ideal.

Finally, my favourite example: imagine you require intensive brain surgery. What profile would you want your surgeon to be? You would probably want someone who is a 'C' (high attention to detail) and an 'S' (slows down when under pressure to perform a task). You would not want a 'D' as your surgeon, as they speed up to get the task done quickly with the only focus on the end result (skipping over detail).

I have no 'D' (or bull) traits. But, as a business owner, sometimes difficult decisions need to be made quickly and effectively (for example, firing an employee or pulling someone up for performance related issues). I *can* do these tasks, but go home at the end of the day exhausted as the tasks were not allowing me to operate in my natural style. For my husband Aaron, who is a high 'D' and very little 'I', if he spends an entire day delivering presentations and interacting with people, he comes home equally exhausted.

What makes a good company **great** is understanding DiSC and ensuring that there is an equal balance of profiles across the entire company. By knowing your team's natural working tendencies, you can start utilising their strengths and weaknesses, and can unite team members so that they can operate as one to achieve the common goal. Having a team of 'peacocks' sounds great in theory (and would create a very loud, talkative and social office), but how much work would actually get done?

For us, delivering projects takes the entire team. Every single person has an important role to play in every single project. By utilising DiSC profiling, developing roles that suit styles, and assigning tasks that are natural to those styles, we have created a team where everyone is respected, understood and working in their natural style.

Our peacocks (I types – sales and design) initially engage with the client, selling and designing their new office space. They then pass the project onto our owls (C types – the estimators) who have the analytical approach and attention to detail to make sure nothing has been missed. The project is won and our sheep (S types) and owls (project administrators) follow our systems, review the contracts, and capture all the key details. The project is then handed over to the peacocks and 'baby' bulls (D types – project managers) who drive the project to completion (remember, bulls focus on the end result). Once the project is completed, the peacocks get excited, flap their feathers and can't wait to see the client's reaction, the bulls are already onto the next project, and the sheep and owls are finalising the back end and cross checking the detail. What a great combination styles!

"Baby bulls?" you ask. In our business, we refer to Aaron as the 'big bull' as he scores the highest percentage of 'D' throughout our team. If we hire another high D person in such a small team, we run the risk of having two bulls in the pen. Horns would be raging, they would argue and create conflict. It would never work. We have made this mistake in the past – it didn't last long! You might have worked in an environment with two or more D types: it can be very unpleasant when they clash!

Teams and seating
Let's take it to the next level!

If your seating plan reflects the DiSC® profiles, you may be able to stimulate the right culture in your office. If you get this right at the beginning, you will save a lot of time, disruption and heartache when you hire new staff. Think about and map out where you would like your teams to be based within the office. For example, if you surround the owls (C type who prefer quiet surrounds and concentration) with peacocks (I type), it is not going to be very harmonised. Similarly, if you place the peacocks in their own offices, they are not going to be comfortable for longer periods of time as they naturally enjoy being surrounded by people (it's like not inviting them to a party!).

Managing personality differences and conflicts
The rewarding part of implementing DiSC® into your work environment is the mutual understanding that all team members start to have for one another. Everyone starts to appreciate each other for their differences and work together as a team.

- D Type

    When the bulls are under pressure, they don't have time for pleasantries. This might come across as offensive! Leave the bulls alone to focus on their tasks without unnecessary interruptions. Bulls are usually also the final decision makers. When communicating options with bulls, save the detail and summarise the two best options and let them make the choice. Remember, their biggest fear is losing control.

- I Type

    When the peacocks are too loud, the owls and sheep find it hard to concentrate. But, because they never want to offend anyone, the bulls will be the ones that ask the peacocks to be quiet. Remember to never go out for lunch without the peacocks, they will get offended as they thrive on social contact.

- S Type

    The sheep are born followers, so be cautious putting them in a leading role where quick decisions are required. They are the backbone supporters in every team. They love instructions, routine and consistency and dislike change. If you are moving offices or desks, ensure that you communicate this with the sheep thoroughly and give them enough notice.

- C Type

    Owls crave detail and slow down when under pressure, so bulls need to learn to give owls enough information so that they can perform their tasks, and not to rush them to completion. The owls cross check and execute the detail that the bull doesn't have time for. You need these people. Allow them time and space to process!

Once your team learns how to interpret each other's behaviours, they will naturally extend this skill and adapt their communication styles to match clients. This will leave your clients feeling more understood and engaged with, which will ultimately increase sales and improve your business!

In our office, not a day goes by that someone doesn't relate the DiSC® profile or animal association to a particular trait of a person – whether it is telling the peacocks to quieten down, or taking a phone call from a bull client and knowing it is best to allow them to make the decision. For us, it's been a real game changer!

Tips to consider when discussing DiSC®

- There are no right or wrong profiles.

- If applicants 'lie' in the test by recording answers we 'want to hear', the results will generally come back invalid and will have to be redone. (This will depend on the tool you use.)

- Most people are a combination of two or three profiles.

- While the DiSC profile is a contributing factor to employment (and for us one slice of the 'pizza'), it should not be the only deciding factor.

- Someone's DiSC profile does not stop them from tackling a task outside of their natural style, it just might require more energy. (Though they shouldn't be doing these tasks long term.)

Reviewing the DiSC® results

Let's get back to recruitment! Once the DiSC® assessments have been returned by the applicants, we review all the profiles. We already know the profile we want for the role and now we have the results! This is where the truth comes out. It is scary how accurate they can be!

TIP

In an interview setting, it is very common for a candidate to show more I traits than what their natural profile has. This is because they are in an environment where they are forced to interact with people and sell themselves to get the position.

We plan the interviews in advance to make sure we can include questions around the DiSC assessment and profiling traits to confirm what the profile is telling us. Some assessment tools provide follow up questions to ask the candidate during the interview.

At this stage of the process, we already know a lot about each candidate's traits, work habits, motivations, development areas, and self-perceptions. We are also aware of their 'natural style' (i.e. their natural behaviour and the actual person that will be showing up to work each day) and their 'adaptive styles' (how they adapt their behaviour to work better within a specific situation).

STEP SEVEN
FIRST INTERVIEW

The first round of interviews is for those applicants who satisfy all the criteria and have successfully made it through every round of the recruitment process.

We **call** the candidates who have been shortlisted for an interview to let them know. We then send a **tailored email** advising them of the interview details. In this email, we also request that they bring certain items to the interview, including a **GREEN HIGHLIGHTER**.

INVITATION TO INTERVIEW EMAIL TEMPLATE	WHAT WE ARE LOOKING FOR
Good Morning/Afternoon [**Name of Candidate**]. Thank you for applying to [**Company Name**]. Your application for the [**role**] position stood out to us and we would like to invite you for an interview at our office on [**date**] at [**time**]. Our office is located at [**address**]. Parking [**is/is not**] available on-site. You will meet with our [**list team and position**] and have the chance to discuss the responsibilities of the position and learn more about our company. Please bring a copy of the vision, mission and values document, a form of photo identification, and a green highlighter to the interview. If you have any questions feel free to give me a call on [**phone number**]. We look forward to discussing the position further with you.	Was interviewee on time and did they bring the requested items, specifically a green highlighter, to the interview? (We do this to test whether the candidate will go out of their way to obtain the highlighter, and if they can follow instructions.) Did the candidate take ownership and complete the task as requested? Or, did they make an excuse and blame others for their failure to deliver? I might sound crazy, but if it's down to the top two candidates and only one has brought a green highlighter, then it may become a deciding factor.

Interview Structure

Make sure that you follow a simple interview structure to keep the conversation flowing. Keeping to an interview structure will be particularly useful if multiple interviewers are sitting on the panel, as it will limit jumping between different topics and different people asking their own set of questions.

A simple structure may include:

- Questions and discussion about the candidate (obtaining and discussing basic personal information and job history).

- Questions around the specific position (clarifying skillset and determining experience).

- Discussion of culture (reviewing the company, culture and team).

- Questions relating to the candidate's DiSC® profile (if you have the assessment at that point in time).

- Canine or trick questions (see bonus section below).

TIP

Remember to ask lots of open ended questions and request examples so that the candidate can justify their answers! You really, really, really want to find out if what you can offer suits the candidates career goals and aspirations – the last thing you want is to hire someone who's expectations weren't met!

STEP EIGHT
REFERENCE CHECKS

The interview went well and you have a good gut feeling. Why bother getting reference checks?

Calling references is vital. Each step of the recruitment process contributes to the bigger picture. You should never make a decision without first checking all of the facts or circumstances.

You want to obtain at least two references from direct supervisors or the business owners. Don't accept references from colleagues, friends, or indirect team members. They will not usually have overseen the candidate's work and can give very biased opinions. Remember, no one will put down a bad referee.

Ask people in your network whether they know (or know someone that may know) the candidate. Search for honest feedback and speak with mutual suppliers, colleagues or connections. This is where the truth will lie.

Prepare for the reference calls by writing out a list of questions (an example template has been included in the Interactive Book). A great question to include is, "if a suitable position became available would you re-hire this candidate?" Listen for any hesitation and follow up with, "why?"

STEP NINE
INTERVIEW TWO

Reference checks are glowing, you still have that good gut feeling, and the other steps in the process are starting to align. I always suggest (and particularly for the more senior positions) that a second interview is arranged.

The focus of this interview is to get to know the *person*, not the applicant. The first interview can be nerve-racking. The applicant is trying to impress you and may portray themselves as someone you want them to see, rather than who they really are.

The second interview is really important to start seeing an applicant's true personality come through. This is a great time to review the DiSC® results again and introduce the applicant to other people in the team. You could ask additional team members to sit in on the interview for further insight.

Depending on the person and position, you could consider inviting the candidate and their partner (if they have one) out to dinner or lunch, in lieu of scheduling a second formal interview. This is a great way to get to know the candidate better and will give you an insight into their life outside of work. By your second meeting, a candidate's real personality will start to shine.

'THE TOUR'

We have a joke in our office that if a candidate makes the office tour, then it is likely they will get the job.

If the second interview goes well, we will invite the candidate for a tour of the office, introducing them to the staff along the way and showing them the facilities. *Every* single detail of this tour is meticulously planned. From who greets them at the door, to who gives the tour.

Usually, we will make sure that a female member of staff greets the candidate at the door. They will be able to use their 'feminine intuition' to get an instant read on the candidate from their handshake, clothes, and mannerisms.

Once the candidate leaves, we ask our team for their feedback and first impressions. Though they will only have had a short introduction, they will be able to say whether candidate seems like a good cultural fit for the office. Some people pick up on things we haven't seen in the interview. Plus, it gives

BONUS SECTION
What breed of canine are you?

In every interview we ask, "If you were a canine, what breed would you be and why?" This question throws off even the most prepared candidates.

We aren't really interested in the breed of dog. It is the *'why'* that is the interesting part. In each candidate's answer, they describe their personality and who they are without even realising it (their subconscious starts speaking). We have tested this theory many times and it definitely works. Plus, it's a bit of fun and light heartedness in the interview!

We once had a man interview for a site position where we needed a strong personality. His answer to the canine question was "pit bull." His 'why' was "due to their aggressive and demanding nature." When he got the job, he *definitely* showed traits of a pit bull. This worked incredibly well, as he needed to take charge and be fierce.

Remember, it is the *why* that is the most important part of the question, not the breed of dog. I had a candidate describe themselves as a labrador, being loyal and friendly. However, someone else labelled the same breed as being lazy and lethargic.

There are many different questions interviewers can ask to determine if a candidate is the right fit for them. The interviewer can find out the applicant's personality type and the soft skills they possess, such as whether they have potential to grow within the company or if they are a good cultural fit. Some other questions you may like to consider are:

What was the last skill you learned and how did you learn it?

The answer to this question should demonstrate how the candidate takes on tasks, whether they are a self-starter, and if they are motivated to find answers on their own. You will also gain insight into whether the candidate is likely to seek professional development to further their skills for the position they are applying for.

What would your friends say about you?

This is another good question to get the truth out of candidates. By asking what their *friends* think (rather than what *they* think), a candidate will be able to describe their personality traits more easily and with more clarity (some people struggle describing themselves, so this is a little trick question). They might say that they are the clown of the group, the friend that everyone goes to for advice, or the person that everyone depends on. These answers will tell you a lot about a candidate's nature and the way they work with others.

If you were an animal, what would you be and why?

This is similar to the canine question. The answer will give you direct insight into the person's personality and behaviours. You wouldn't want someone who is a mouse (timid and shy) to work in sales. They just wouldn't fit!

What is your dream company to work for and why?

Sometimes candidates are very honest and will name drop your largest competitor. Do you want to invest time and money into someone who is using you and your business as a 'stepping stone'? Other candidates might describe their dream company, only for you to discover that what they think they have applied for is not your business model. For example, at Future Fitouts we know that building high rises and designing hospitality fitouts are not our core spaces. So, if we had a candidate openly wanting to work in these sectors, they may never be satisfied in their role without that exposure.

What other questions can you think of? Take your time and write them here. Be as creative as you like.

_____

_____

_____

_____

_____

_____

_____

the candidate the opportunity to experience the office vibe and meet the team prior to starting (if they are successful).

STEP TEN
POLICE CHECK AND HEALTH QUESTIONNAIRE

Getting the candidate to deselect!

The entire recruitment process is based around getting the candidate to deselect themselves. At every stage, you want to test them so that only the strong are left standing.

The police check is a great opportunity for candidates to deselect themselves, as an applicant with a police record will remove themselves from the talent pool. This is a much better outcome than hiring someone only to find out that they have a criminal conviction further down the track.

It is also a good idea to have candidates complete a health questionnaire. The main aim of this document is to protect you as an employer. Though a person's health status may not inhibit them from fulfilling the requirements of a role, it is always a good idea for an employer to be aware of and understand any underlying medical conditions of staff so that they can be managed appropriately.

STEP 11
MAKE AN OFFER (AND CELEBRATE)

Congratulations!

The hard work is done! It is now time to make an offer to the successful candidate and celebrate!

We always have our team in the background when we call to make an offer. We put the candidate on speaker (after we have made sure it is a suitable time to chat) and then offer them the position. Once they accept, we hit the gong and our team cheers and celebrates with the soon to be employee!

Once you have spoken with the candidate, you will then need to follow up in writing to confirm the offer of employment and fulfil the legal requirements. Send the candidate the employment contracts, induction documents, and administrative forms to be completed. I recommend you engage a good human resources solicitor or work with a company like Employsure to guide you on the legalities of hiring new staff and ensure that it is done correctly.

Looking to get some advice? Head to the Interactive Book for your referral code for Employsure.

STEP 12
NOTIFY UNSUCCESSFUL CANDIDATES

It is equally important to notify the unsuccessful candidates, particularly those who completed a number of the steps in the recruitment process. People appreciate a response. Just because an applicant has not made it through this time, does not mean that an opportunity won't open up in the future that is more suitable for them. Never burn your bridges. It is your company's reputation on the line. If applicants have taken the time to apply, they deserve a response.

We have hired a number of candidates that weren't suitable for the role they applied for. Through open communication we were able to find other positions in the company that they now thrive in!

> *Talent will start coming to you! Be in the position to turn down, instead of needing to hire.*

Never Skip a Step!

Hopefully you are thinking how great and thorough this process is. But, you are probably also considering the time it takes.

Our record for getting through our entire recruitment process is **three days** from advertising the position, to having the team member **start**. I credit this to the system! Imagine having a key player resign and being able to fill the role within three days! Of course, this is not always possible when working around set time frames, like notice periods. On average our success rate is two to three weeks for the full process to be done correctly.

We will **always** wait to hire the right person, rather than hiring the wrong person because they are available. On one occasion, we advertised the same role three times and waited five months to get the right person. Let the system do the work for you and you will eventually find the right people.

In the next chapter, I will discuss onboarding and training in more detail. You want to make sure that you set your new team member up for success from day one!

Setting up for Success

> **❝** *Hire slowly and fire fast"*
> *– Ronnie Apteker*

THE ONBOARDING PROCESS

At Future Fitouts, we make sure that **all** of our employees have everything they need to be comfortable, safe, and efficient at work. All new employees receive an employee handbook containing information about the business.

We like to go the **extra mile** and make an employee's first day memorable. The **night before** a new employee commences, we make it a priority to email them some information about the business and what to expect on their first day. We confirm their start time, whether parking is available, a **power of positive language sheet**, the Future Fitouts Cheat Sheet (a document that contains little insights into our culture and office jokes), and an overall welcome to the business. We let them know how excited we are to have them join our team and that there is nothing to be nervous about. This helps reassure them that they are coming into a welcoming environment.

The subject line of the email is "Sweet dreams and see you tomorrow," and the body contains wording along the lines of;

> To: [Candidate Name]
>
> Subject: Sweet dreams and see you tomorrow
>
> We hope that you are excited for your first day and trust this email calms any nerves you may have.
>
> We attach some of our orientation documents to give you an idea of what to expect on your first day.
>
> Get a good night's sleep and we will see you tomorrow at 9 am.
>
> Kind regards,
>
> Lauren and Aaron

SETTING UP FOR SUCCESS

First days are very overwhelming: new team, new systems, new travel route to work. Everything is information overload!

FIRST DAY, FIRST IMPRESSION

Once you have recruited your new team or team member, you need to induct them into the culture and operations of your business.

Do you remember your first day at a new job? Did you feel nervous to meet new people and learn new systems? Chances are, you did. The way you induct a team member on their first day, week, and month leaves them with a lasting impression of your company and sets up an expectation of the culture you have created.

It is important that everyone feels welcome and a part of the team as soon as they start. At Future Fitouts, we have created an induction and onboarding system (surprise, surprise) to give team members the best start to their career with us, from day one. Having a system in place that inducts a team member thoroughly ensures that they are ready to hit the ground running and start making your company money.

If your new employee comes in on their first day and sees that you are prepared for their arrival (maybe you have organised a desk for them, activated their passwords, or printed their business cards), they will instantly feel valued. Having these things ready also indicates that your company is organised and efficient, and has the same expectations of everyone in it.

Take the time to introduce new team members to the rest of the staff and show them around the office. Point out where the kitchenette and bathroom are and let them know that they are free to make coffee or tea whenever they like. Show them how things are done and take them through some of the systems that are in place.

Put yourself in your new employee's shoes and try not to underestimate the number of new things that they are learning. Remember that they are stepping into a new job, with new people that they do not know. Give them a first day that they will brag about for years to come by showing them that you care as soon as they step through the door!

We use this First Day Checklist to ensure our new team members are welcomed properly on their first day.

- ☐ Have IT been notified and are logins and passwords ready?

- ☐ Have their business cards been printed?

- ☐ Has a layout of desks with corresponding names and titles been printed to give to them? (This will save the employee the embarrassment of trying to remember everyone's names on their first day.)

- ☐ Has a warm welcome been organised, such as a team morning tea, personalised card, or little gift? (Our employees receive a personalised card from Aaron and I and a small gift.)

- ☐ Are existing team members aware of the new employee's start date? (There is nothing worse than someone not knowing a new person is starting and that they are responsible for training them.)

- ☐ Has the new employee's workstation (desk, chair, and stationery) been set up?

- ☐ Do they need any company property (phone, laptop, or car)? If so, has this been organised?

- ☐ Does the induction system set the new employee up for success?

FIRST THREE MONTHS AND PROBATION PERIOD

Anyone can be on their best behaviour during an interview. This is also true of the first three months of an employee's contract.

It is not hard for someone to put on a persona for those initial 12 weeks. They are learning, everything is new and they are yet to master their role. This all nicely coincides with the standard three month probation period contained in general employment contracts. For this reason alone, we always extend our probation period to six months, at a minimum.

Generally, you will start to see the real person between the four and six month mark. Their personality will start showing through and you will begin to understand how they handle stress and interact with team members.

Did you know that almost 30% of people will leave a job within three months of getting it?[4]

All that effort in recruiting and training to have *30% of people* leave within *three months* of starting?! This is why the recruitment process is so important!

Set the candidate up for success on their first day. By inducting new team members thoroughly, addressing any questions or concerns swiftly, and conducting reviews regularly, we give our employees the best chance at becoming long term members of our team.

We adopted and implemented an idea from Eben Pagan, an entrepreneur who was interviewed as part of Tony Robbins's segment, 'How to Hire Superstars'.[5] As part of our induction process, the new employee sends a daily afternoon email to their direct manager and to Aaron and I. On the employee's second day, and for the next 15 (or 30) days, she/he is asked to send a quick email addressing the following questions:

1. **What have you achieved?**

2. **What are your challenges?**

3. **What questions do you have?**

This should only take five or ten minutes and will give the new hire a chance to reflect upon their day and performance, triggering any questions that they may have. It also acts as a prompt for us to teach the new employee aspects of the business that we may have forgotten.

PART SIX

CULTIVATE LEADERSHIP AND WELLNESS

(See, positivity works!)

Being a Leader

A good leader leads by example.

The next few pages will take you through how you can be the best leader possible, while still running a successful business. Try things that challenge you to take your leadership to a whole new level.

One of the most important aspects of being a good leader is the ability to motivate your team. Bringing out the leader within you will inspire your staff to do the same. Here are some ways that you can motivate staff, while also making them feel wanted, safe and part of a family. This will increase productivity and happiness within the office.

The word 'leader' and 'manager' are often thrown around interchangeably, but it is important that you understand the differences between the two.

LEADER	MANAGER
o Coaches and guides the team	o Provides detail on how to achieve individual tasks
o Inspires the team	o Directs the team
o Considers the 'big picture'	o Focuses on set goals
o Looks to the future	o Works towards current targets
o Focuses on developing people within the company	o Focuses on achieving goals within the company
o Drives new ideas	o Implements the execution of new ideas
o Does not need to be authority figure	o Power is formally delegated to her/him

People want to work for an inspiring and approachable leader; someone who understands them, focuses on individual strengths (and not weaknesses), a person that is inspiring and leads with integrity and compassion. A leader is someone who guides the team through thick and thin.

We want all of our team to feel safe and comfortable. We have tried to create an environment where staff are able to directly come and talk to us, openly and honestly about anything. We want our staff to willingly share ideas without fear of judgement and know that their opinions are valued.

> *What does it mean to be a leader? "Anyone can be a leader…but being a leader is a privilege not a right."*

Being a leader means you are **real** with your employees. You are **approachable** and are a **great listener.** You have **emotions** and take **ownership** of mistakes. You need to show your employees that you are **still learning** and **challenge** everyone to be the best version of themselves.

What can you do to be a great leader?

1. **Define clear goals**

    If the company, team and individual goals are ambiguous and the expectations of positions are not clear, how can you expect your people to achieve? Time is wasted when priorities have not been explained and the employee is too afraid seek clarification. As the leader, it is your job to create specific goals for each team and team member to work towards so that everyone is operating towards a common target. A team wants to feel like they are working towards something big, together! If you have not heard of a BHAG (Big Hairy Audacious Goal), do yourself a favour and read up on it.

2. **Showing up for the 'right game'**

    A leader needs to be piloting the plane, keeping the business (or team) on course, and navigating the crew through any difficult weather conditions. Imagine a cockpit. The pilot has a clear map showing the destination. Although the plane may go slightly off course, the pilot's role is to bring it back on route.

A leader in business is no different. The leader needs to know the end goal or outcome and be agile and flexible in bringing the team along with them.

A good leader will also ensure the team is showing up to the 'right game'. A business coach we had for some time explained this concept to us using a sports analogy. He said, "you are all playing sport, but are you playing the *same sport*, or are you showing up to a tennis match with football boots?" It is important for a leader to make sure everyone is on the same page and working towards the common goal. It is one thing for the leader to know the direction of the company, but it's another for them to be able to communicate and lead the rest of the team to it.

3. Lead with integrity

Trust, honesty and integrity: three of my biggest values which have guided every decision we have made in business over the years. Be truthful with your team. Business is hard, but you will gain more respect from your team if you openly share some of the issues the business may be facing.

4. Fit the oxygen mask first

Continuing with the 'plane analogy'; always fit your own oxygen mask first before helping others.

In other words, look after *you* first by practising a weekly self care routine. It might sound selfish, but how can you bring your best self to work if you are drained, exhausted, and stressed out? How can you make good business decisions if your mind is not clear?

We have all been there (myself included). I've had many sleepless nights, long hours and high stress events. But, if there is one thing I have learned (and it has taken me a *long* time), it is that I need to put myself first!

Human performance strategist and leadership coach Andrew May has written a wonderful article on this. Andrew's detailed recovery strategy explains the various reasons why downtime, going slow, and taking a break is so important. You can find the article in full in the Interactive Book.

5. Create a pleasant office

As already discussed, the work environment is a crucial element to keeping your team motivated and happy. (Refer to Parts Two and Three for tips on this.)

6. Provide self-development opportunities

When you offer employees the opportunity to learn more, you are giving them the freedom to obtain new skills which will benefit their personal and professional development, as well as your business. Employees will feel more confident in their knowledge of the industry, which translates into higher productivity in the workplace. It's a win win!

7. Encourage collaboration

Give team members the opportunity to suggest changes to the workplace or ideas to improve culture. This will foster healthy discussions and some great ideas may be raised that you haven't even considered (plus, it means you don't have to come up with the solution for everything). As mentioned earlier, I recommend reading *Culture is Everything* by Tristan White for some great insights into team ideas and creating a contagious culture.

8. Remember that we are only humans

Punishing your staff for a mistake will only discourage them and create further divide in the team relationship. When employees make an error or fail to deliver a desired outcome, take it as a learning opportunity. Accept the mistake (that is, of course, if it's not the same mistake being repeated over and over again) and look for the opportunity for improvement. Consider what you and your team can do differently, what was learned, whether more training is needed, and if a system should be updated. By creating an open, honest and supportive environment, the team are more likely to come to you with mistakes and assist in finding the solution.

9. **Trust your team**

If you have provided the right tools, support, training and environment, you must trust that your team are able to do their jobs. Provide staff with their work outcomes and give them the freedom to achieve.

Micromanaging and clock watching staff creates a toxic environment. If a team member is finished their work ten minutes earlier than their finish time, allow them to leave early every once in a while.

10. **Schedule fun**

You can always find time to include fun in your schedule. Make this a priority every day!

Plan little treats and events that make your staff smile. Think about the personalities of your employees and schedule activities that you know they will enjoy. As reiterated throughout this entire book; when people are relaxed and happy, they will be more inclined to work harder and be more productive.

11. **Say THANK YOU!**

When was the last time you personally thanked your team for showing up to work? It's simple and doesn't cost a thing, but is *rarely* done. Thanking staff regularly is a sign of respect and leads to increased confidence and morale in the workplace. Leading a team that feels appreciated will not only benefit their mood, but will increase productivity and efficiency. Take one minute to go thank a team member and genuinely mean it.

TEAM DYNAMICS

As a leader, it is essential that you recognise and nurture the dynamics within your team if you want your business to succeed. How your team communicates and collaborates with one another impacts how their work gets done, which ultimately affects the wider organisation. Your staff don't need to be best friends, but they do need to be able to work together to achieve the common goal.

Ignoring the dynamics within a team can lead to conflict, reduce productivity and degrade culture. As a leader, you must understand the importance of team dynamics so you can mitigate any problems as they arise.

The first step is to get to know each member of your team as an individual person, their communication and behavioural styles, and who they are at work and home. (If you have conducted a DiSC® assessment, you should already have most of this information!) If you don't know where to start, take them out for a casual coffee or lunch and start building a relationship.

Secondly, as a leader it is important that you understand the different stages of teamwork so that you can effectively manage any issues that crop up. The 1965 group development model proposed by Bruce Tuckman – forming, storming, norming, performing[1] – outlines the process that a team goes through to complete a task.

1. **Forming** is the first stage of a group project and involves the team orienting themselves with the task and each other. The team members meet for the first time and begin to form and allocate roles and responsibilities. During this phase, the group might start outlining how they will approach the task at hand.

2. The group then moves on to **storming;** the hardest part of the process. During this phase, team members start voicing their opinions and begin to get to know one another. Some team members may experience "feelings of inadequacy"[2] and might wonder who in the team will "support or undermine them."[3] This can be a difficult stage to work through with frustrations amongst team members.

3. During the **norming** stage, the group begins to develop cohesion and starts to work together. The team collaborates to focus on the common goal and will have ironed out any team differences.

4. The **performing** stage is where it all comes together. The team members will be working efficiently and channelling their "energy… into the task"[4] so that it can be completed to a high level. This is the ultimate goal for every team.

In 1977, Tuckman added a fifth stage to his model – '**adjourning**'.[5] This is the final stage in which the task is completed and the group may dissolve.

As a leader, you must be able to recognise that group projects don't just 'happen', but involve a team progressing through these set developmental stages. Once you understand this, you will be better equipped to navigate how and when certain tasks should be allocated and completed. By knowing which stage the group is at during a project, you can offer advice, be the voice of authority, or step in to assist.

SHOW YOUR EQ

Emotional intelligence, or emotional quotient (EQ), is something that is learned with experience over time. Our EQ helps measure self-awareness, recognise our own and others' sensitivities, and regulates empathy. As a team leader, you must show that you are self-aware and lead by example through your own EQ.

Below are some easy steps to expand your own EQ that you can share with your team.

Manage your emotions

When you manage your emotions, you can stop negativity obstructing the production of great work by compartmentalising what is triggering you and focussing on what can be achieved. A great way to do this is to recognise when you are feeling overwhelmed and take a break. Manage this properly and be self-aware. Never take out your frustrations on staff or the people around you. Calmness is key.

It is important to remind yourself to breathe throughout the day. You might like to schedule ten minutes every day where your staff come together to complete breathing exercises. I have a reminder set at 2 pm every day to stop and take five slow, long, and deep breaths.

☐ **Choose your words carefully**

Speak intelligently. Avoid using profanities or angry tones in the office. If you feel frustrated and your language is becoming aggressive, take five minutes away from the office to unwind and calm down. Remember, you are leading by example.

☐ **Be empathic**

Being empathetic is putting yourself in another person's shoes so that you can appreciate their perspective. Rather than reacting to a situation, you should try to understand where the other person is coming from by listening to them and responding calmly. Practise doing this often so that it becomes second nature.

Empathy is innate for many, but for some, it must be learned. If you need to increase your empathy, try role playing. Pick a scenario and act it out. By adopting a role, you will be able to understand how someone in that position would feel.

☐ **Understand your own personal triggers**

Once you learn what stresses you out, you will be able to recognise when things are getting too much. Share what triggers you with your team to let them know that sometimes you will get stressed. Know when you are feeling overwhelmed and practise stress management exercises to keep calm.

☐ **Employees have family too**

You never know if someone is going through something and is experiencing a difficult situation in their private lives. They may not feel comfortable sharing it, but do their best to show up professionally and hide their emotions while at work.

Remember that your team have families, personal lives and are juggling priorities too. Look after them like they're your own family. If they have regularly been staying back to work on a project, offer them a day off or shout a weekend getaway to really show your appreciation.

THE POWER OF POSITIVE LANGUAGE

Positive language is extremely important, especially in the workplace. It encourages personable connections and improves the collective atmosphere and morale in the office. A positive culture will promote healthy and happy mindsets so that everyone can succeed.

The diagram below explains the impact that language has on us day-to-day.

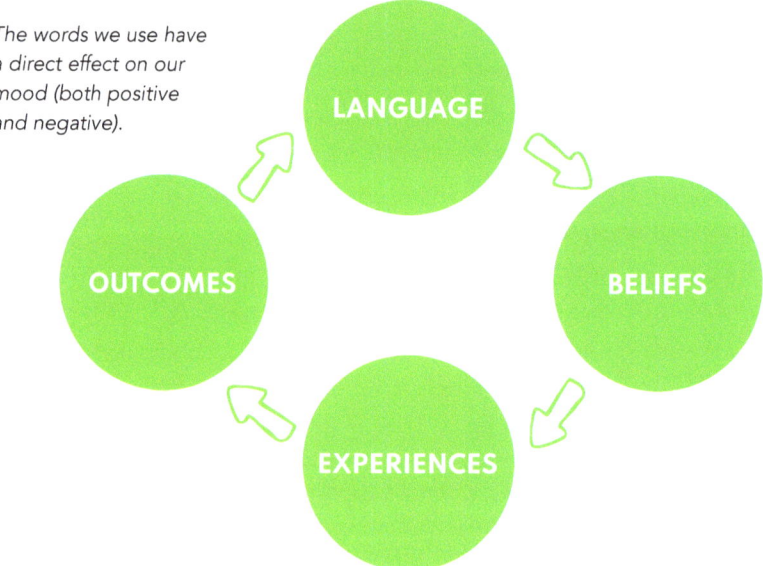

The words we use have a direct effect on our mood (both positive and negative).

- Language carries and encourages beliefs.
- Beliefs create and influence experiences.
- Experiences influence outcomes.
- Outcomes reinforce beliefs.
- Beliefs are carried through language, and it starts all over again!

Once you are aware of this progression, you can change it. The cycle always begins with language.

Place the diagram opposite in your space to show your team how they can each promote a positive work environment.

1. **Feeling**

   Take charge of your own emotions.

2. **Thinking**

   Make a *commitment* (not just a mere effort) to only think positive thoughts.

3. **Action**

   Encourage positivity through your actions.

4. **Feedback**

   Give positive and constructive feedback to staff, or offer support to those who need it. Provide feedback to yourself by reflecting and reassessing how you can maintain positivity in the office.

Practise positive words

We have probably all been around that one person who constantly complains. They're tired and there's too much work to do, the office is *freezing* and someone ate the last biscuit from the break room! It is draining, not to mention, completely unproductive.

Never be that person! Instead, make the conscious effort to use positive language whenever you are in the office. If you hear or experience something negative, try turning it into a positive: "at least we get to work in air conditioning and the boss provides biscuits!"

By doing this, you will promote a positive belief system, which, in turn, will generate more positivity within the team. This benefits everyone.

Let's do a test. Say the following out loud:

"I will try."

Your brain thinks, *I'll give it a go*. There is a hesitation and a lack of belief that you will actually complete the task.

Now say,

"I will do it!"

Did you feel the difference? By using words that communicate strong and affirmative action, your mind believes the message more readily.

I have listed some common words and phrases opposite to help you increase your positive language at work.

At Future Fitouts, we use the word 'clients' as opposed to 'customers'. A 'client' indicates a long-term relationship, whereas a 'customer' is considered a one-off. Your business wants *clients*, so make sure that you are using this language.

My number one pet hate is when people greet me with "morning" in a monotone voice. What, are we in *mourning*? No! The morning is *good*, so why not say it like that?

"Good morning!"

Now, that is a friendly and happy greeting, wouldn't you agree?

Another pet hate of mine (a default response of many people, *particularly* Aussies) is the phrase "no worries." When someone replies this way, the listener hears the word 'worry' and subconsciously, their brain becomes uneasy.

And the last one (I promise): "please don't hesitate to contact me." This is common in email signatures. My brain sees the words 'don't contact me' and immediately 'hesitates' to make contact. Invite the recipient to reply by amending the wording to "feel free to contact me." This is a subtle yet powerful change.

> **PHONE TIP**
>
> Do you want someone to remember your name during a phone call? Then make sure it is the last thing they hear!
>
> Answer the phone with, "welcome to [company name], this is [your name]."
>
> If you end with "[your name] speaking" or "how may I help you," you have reduced the chance of the caller remembering your name.

POSITIVE	NEGATIVE
Will: Often used to positively commit to a task. Very empowering.	**Should**: This carries a negative connotation as it is disempowering. Often, the word 'should' is used as an excuse for not doing something.
Won't: This suggests that you are choosing not to do it, rather than that you are unable to do it. Choosing not to do something allows you to hold onto your personal power. This is positive.	**Can't**: Unless it is physically impossible, then you definitely *can* do it. You are just making excuses! Instead, suggest that you are *not able* to do it.
Do it: Suggests that you will commit to the task regardless of the outcome. You are taking the opportunity to learn and do more.	**Try**: Suggests that what has been asked of you is too difficult. Therefore, you are stating that you are not committing to it.
Do your best: Is positively driven and is a statement of empowerment and encouragement.	**Try harder**: Completely negative and holds negative connotations.
And: Builds upon the previous statements by adding to the content or conversation with power and positivity. Does not dismiss anyone else's opinion.	**But (or however)**: Using these dismisses and rebuts everything that was said previously in a sentence. Not positive words to use.

Break the bad habits.
Consciously remind your team members to maintain a positive mindset and use more positive language in the office. Remember, as the leader your actions (or lack thereof) are closely followed and repeated. You might also like to install a board filled with affirmations and positive reminders in the workspace.

At Future Fitouts, we send out an article on positive language to all new employees the day before they start.

Think about…

Why is it when you say to a child "don't do that," they never listen?

It is because they need to know 'why'.

Positive language is extremely beneficial to a child's understanding and can dramatically alter their response to verbal communication. For example, a teacher saying, "It's slippery in here, so running is dangerous" is much more likely to be effective than them simply ordering, "stop running."

This is the same for adults. By changing your choice of words and using positive language, you create a more open and constructive dialogue.

TEAM SLOGANS

Does anyone in your team have a mantra, slogan or mannerism that could be adopted throughout the whole workplace?

When we onboard a team member at Future Fitouts, they receive a copy of the 'FF Way Cheat Sheet' which contains all our sayings and mannerisms (this is different to our values). Not only does this continue to help grow our culture, it also allows new staff to feel part of the team from day one and not miss out on any inside jokes. A few of our mantras:

o   Taking over the world.

o   How do we create 'wow' today?

- Come to me with solutions!
- We are the solution providers.
- The Future Fitouts way.
- Be the bigger person.
- We can do anything, and what if this works?
- Opportunity is everywhere.
- If you're not early, your late!
- 5xP's – Prior preparation prevents poor performance

POSITIVE WORDS
POST THEM EVERYWHERE

There are loads of great words that you can display around the office. If you're not sure where to start, I have included some ideas below that you can print out. You could also check out some wall art shops for posters to place strategically in exposed areas.

Another great idea is to ask a different team member each week to write a positive quote or affirmation on the bathroom mirrors with a whiteboard marker.

I can do that.

Too easy.

My pleasure.

I am pleased you asked.

I will make it happen.

Consider it done.

Certainly can.

Absolutely.

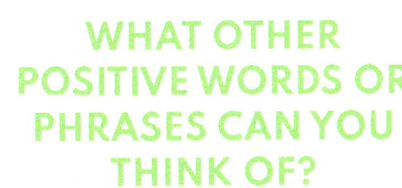

WHAT OTHER POSITIVE WORDS OR PHRASES CAN YOU THINK OF?

Ask this at your next staff meeting and have everyone write down some positive phrases to share with the team.

Showing Love at Work

Have you heard of *The 5 Love Languages* by Gary Chapman?[6] It is a great read that has been revered as the 'relationship bible'.

In his book, Chapman explores the ways in which different people show and receive love. He explains that a person's experience and expression of love can be broken down into five unique categories, known as the 'love languages'. According to Chapman, these include:

1. Receiving Gifts
2. Quality Time
3. Words of Affirmation
4. Acts of Service
5. Physical Touch

While Chapman's book provides fascinating insight into romantic relationships, it is also pertinent to the workplace. In 2007, Chapman released another book with co-author Paul White titled *The 5 Languages of Appreciation in the Workplace*[7] which reinterprets the love languages in a professional context.

So, how you can target and nurture each love language within your workplace so that the whole office benefits? The following suggestions have been adapted from Chapman's book.

1. **Gift Giving**

    Small tokens of appreciation can be hugely uplifting for staff. The gifts you give will depend on your budget, but can be as simple as office snacks, sweets, or ad hoc complimentary team lunches.

    Surprising staff with gifts during the holiday season or to celebrate a job well done is another great way to express genuine appreciation. Adding a touch of personalisation to any gifts you give will show that you care about and value the team member as an individual.

2. Quality Time

Increase the loyalty of your staff by making sure that you set aside quality one on one time to spend with employees who speak this as their love language. This could be in the form of a weekly five minute catch up, or a regular debrief to touch base about personal and professional happenings.

Schedule group events so that everyone can socialise outside of the office. It is much easier for staff to get along if they understand each other on a personal level to some degree. Creating an environment where staff can exchange friendly banter will promote open communication, and make them more likely to remain loyal to the organisation.

3. Words of Affirmation

Reduce cynicism and create an encouraging work environment by using positive speech and regularly telling colleagues how much you appreciate them and the work that they do. This will go a long way towards sustaining a happier and more fulfilled team.

Affirmations and positive language need to come from the top to set an example of how everyone should interact with each other in the workplace. 'Thank you' is a simple but powerful expression that can make a world of difference to an employee's attitude and overall job satisfaction. Try it out. Next time you pass a team member in the office, thank them just for coming to work. You will be surprised how much it means to them!

4. Acts of Service

Do something for your employees that shows your appreciation for them. Make sure any acts of service you deliver are true from the heart, consistent over time, and reflect what is important to your staff.

Offer your employees support by getting on the ground and

getting your hands dirty. This might include assisting team members with tasks that they find difficult. It is important that staff understand you are willing to help, and that they can come to you with anything they need. Your employees should feel like there is never any competition in the office, as everyone is part of a team that supports one another.

> Make The 5 Languages of Appreciation in the Workplace work for you

5. Touch

There are many ways to express appreciation through touch in the workplace. High fiving colleagues to celebrate a job well done, patting someone on the back for reassurance, or shaking another person's hand are all ways that you can express appropriate touch at work.

These simple forms of physical touch should not be forgotten when showing appreciation in the workplace. Remember to always approach touch with caution and gain the other person's consent before engaging in contact.

Each language holds a different level of value depending on the person, so it is worthwhile finding out which is most appreciated by your employees. In saying this, you should strive to show appreciation in all five areas, so that staff can feel completely happy and secure in their roles.

You won't be able to implement every strategy outlined above immediately, especially if there are unresolved issues and tensions in your workplace. Move ahead slowly. By consistently showing appreciation for and to your staff, you will gradually notice a positive shift in the culture and mood of your office.

Your efforts must be habitual and genuine to ensure that staff feel valued. Swap out one off gestures for sustained acts of gratitude, which will have long lasting positive impacts on your staff morale.

Remember that all staff are individuals

> "A happy and productive working environment results in happy staff and better outcomes for our clients!"
> – Lauren Lowe

and will experience 'love languages' differently. Not all languages work on every person.

Random Acts of Kindness

Focus on building a workplace that is filled with people who want to be there because they like your company, stand with your vision, and share your values. You don't want a bunch of people sticking it out just because you pay well!

This is what will take you from being just another boss, to becoming a great and memorable leader. *You* can be that 1% difference for your business!

LITTLE THINGS AND QUICK WINS

Everybody wants recognition for their hard work, so it is important that you show your employees that they are seen and their efforts are being noticed.

According to Glassdoor's 2017 HR and Recruiting Statistics, nearly 80% of employees surveyed would prefer new or additional benefits over a pay rise, and 90% of millennials prefer benefits over a pay increase.[8]

Some of the ways that we like to reward our employees are outlined below. You might like to put some of these ideas in place in your business. They promote a culture that your employees are valued, what they are doing is being recognised, and they are not just another number to fill a seat in your office. These rewards are appreciated and not expected.

Random acts of kindness and thoughtful surprises go so much further than anticipated pay rises and reviews. Here is a list of ideas you can have on hand ready to surprise and thank your team!

MANAGE REMOTE TEAMS

Don't forget about the staff who work remotely, either from home or other offices! These people are still part of your team and deserve the same recognition that you would give the staff who work beside you every day.

Consider including remote team members in a morning huddle, arrange online vouchers or surprise them with a food delivery at home.

INCENTIVE IDEAS

FREE

- ✓ Verbal recognition (team or individual, public or private)
  You might like to recognise particular team members in meetings and let everyone know what a great job they are doing.

- ✓ Thank you notes
  Writing a simple message to thank your staff is an easy way to show your appreciation.

- ✓ Flexibility to work from home
  Working from home costs you nothing (and might even increase an employee's productivity).

- ✓ Pool sick leave with annual leave
  Let employees use accrued sick leave as they would annual leave (i.e. they don't need to be sick).

- ✓ Celebrate birthdays and 'work-aversaries'
  A simple card signed by all staff can make someone feel appreciated and special.

- ✓ Use recognition apps
  There are plenty of applications available that can boost team morale. Use these to send stickers and incentive notes to team members!

LOW COST

- ✓ Chocolate bar, lolly buffet or ice creams in the freezer
  Who doesn't love chocolate or stumbling upon a lolly buffet in the work kitchen?

- ✓ Coffees and drinks
  Arrange a coffee run for the team or offer drinks in the kitchen.

- ✓ Scratchie
  A fun little surprise that will brighten a team member's day.

- ✓ Day off/leave early/start late
  Everyone loves to have an early finish or late start at work!

- ✓ Dinner or movie voucher
  Who doesn't enjoy going out for dinner and a movie. Show them and their family that you care.

- ✓ Car space or transport
  Cover the cost of public transport for a week, or offer a carpark for a period of time.

HIGHER COST

- ✓ Gift card
  Purchasing a gift card for your employee's favourite store is a great way to show them that small wins matter.

- ✓ Holiday or family escape
  Let's face it, if your team are working longer hours it is their family who are making the sacrifice. One of our favourite gifts is the gift of time with loved ones. Shout employees a weekend away, health retreat, or experience so they can create memories with their families.

- ✓ Upgrade phones and laptops
  Why not gift your employees something that will make their lives easier and more productive?

- ✓ Team building session
  This could be fun and casual, or more serious with a learning objective at the end. This is a great way to thank staff for their efforts away from the office.

- ✓ Session with an advisor
  Book a one on one goal setting session with a professional mentor, business coach, trainer, or advisor.

Wellness at Work

We spend a *lot* of time at work. And, as hours grow longer and time outside of work gets smaller, more and more workers in Australia are succumbing to the symptoms of stress and burnout. With the ability to be connected to technology 24/7, this isn't going to change anytime soon. Because of this, promoting the wellbeing of your employees has never been more important.

At Future Fitouts, we make the wellness of our team one of our key priorities. I have included various ways that we promote wellness at work below.

MORNING TEAM RITUAL

Many successful people and top performers have morning rituals. These consist of everything from meditating and journaling, to cold showers, exercising and green smoothies. If you haven't come across this concept before, I encourage you to do some googling and create your own morning power routine.

At Future Fitouts, we took this idea one step further and created a team morning stretch ritual. It lasts around ten minutes (two to three times a week) and helps us bond and strengthen relationships as a team. While we stretch, we go over the tasks for the day, discuss what is happening in our personal lives, or share something that the team don't know about us. It is the one time of day that we can stop and focus on each other and is a great way to kick start the morning.

OUR TEN MINUTE ROUTINE

1. We wake up our lymphatic system with some light flow movement and/or body taping exercises to get the blood flowing to every area of the body.

2. We continue with easy, light stretches that everyone can participate in. Here, team members take turns contributing to a stretch, yoga pose, or body movement.

3. We then complete three slow, deep breaths and actively fill our minds with positive thoughts and breathe out anything that is outside our control.

4. On the third breath, we share (or shout) something that we are grateful for (one of our values). This ends the stretch ritual which leaves us feeling fuelled and ready to start the day.

At times, we have implemented a 'daily huddle'. This is a quick email sent to all team members that outlines our company values, whether we achieved the previous day's priority, how we are going to create 'wow' for someone else, what we are taking ownership of, and recaps our number one focus for the day.

Having this little team routine sets up the day for productivity and togetherness. It gives our team the purpose and structure to produce efficient and effective work, and also gives us time to learn more about each other on a personal note.

What can you do to create a bond within your workplace?

A. Set a purpose for the day or a team goal to work towards.

B. Give each person the chance to share something important.

C. Discuss project statuses and updates.

D. Outline specific team goals to encourage outcomes.

E. Provide one another with client updates and information.

You decide how casual or formal you would like your morning huddle or team bonding session to be. You can choose to make it fun – allowing people to take turns to speak and turning it into a game – or, you can follow a more rigid structure. Whatever you do will encourage team spirit and help your staff feel heard, part of a team, and up to date with important dates and events.

DAILY EXERCISE

Daily exercise is an important part of anyone's day, and incorporating it into the office will benefit all staff (particularly those who are time poor). If you have the space, you might like to include an area within the office for a gym or workout room. Many large organisations have a gym accessible to staff any time they wish. Having some time in the morning to do a stretch and some on-the-spot jogging will help get staff moving (which is important if they spend all day sitting). Providing options for individual or team exercise at work is a great way to build rapport and a healthy mindset for all.

GONG SOUND MEDITATION

Remember that gong I mentioned in Part Three? Well, using it as part of an office meditation will do wonders for team wellness and morale. Gong master and sound practitioner, Leith James, believes that the benefits of gong sound meditation speak for themselves, and can include reduced absenteeism and staff turnover, higher productivity, and better team relations at work.[9]

Gong meditation combines the healing properties of meditation with the medicinal impacts of sound. According to Leith, sound has the power to reduce stress, improve problem solving abilities, and stimulate calmer and clearer thinking.

Gong meditation has a cumulative effect, meaning that regular practice will increase a person's ability to deal with stress over time. So, what better way to create long-term office calmness than by scheduling regular gong meditation sessions for you and your staff? Not only will meditation sessions help release office tension, they will also give your team the opportunity to bond by participating in an activity together.

If you are interested in learning more about gong sound meditation, head to the Interactive Book for a link to Leith's blog.

GRATITUDE WALL

A gratitude wall is a great way to utilise wall space for a positive outcome. Your staff can take a moment to place a card, a note, or post it on the wall that states what it is they are grateful for. You can ask your team to add a new note whenever you choose. It is a great visual reminder that every day is a good day when you are grateful.

Having a gratitude wall will also ensure that your staff feel that it is okay to bring the gratitudes of their lives into the professional space. They might like to put family photos up or pictures of their pets. As the leader, you might consider including positive and powerful words. This wall will help maintain a healthy and happy mindset for everyone passing by.

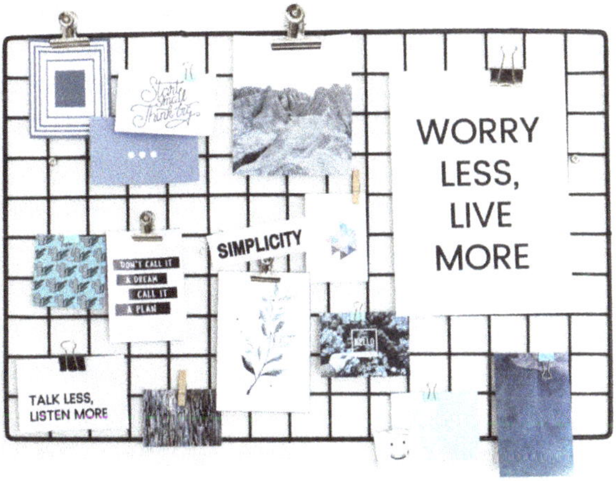

Any Excuse to Celebrate!

Celebrate the little things and quick wins. Have your team help you compile a list of what they consider quick wins, and then choose a celebratory action, like a fun dance or special shake to do when a win occurs.

Everybody – regardless of what they say – likes to feel special on their birthday. And everybody should have that feeling on their special day. At Future Fitouts, each one of our team members is given a day off for their birthday to use on a day of their choice.

However, this is not limited to birthdays. Other important days like start date anniversaries, end of probation periods, and company milestones should all be celebrated. We make a big deal of all these events and go that little bit extra to make our staff feel special. After all, celebrating together brings the team closer and builds connections and trust.

SEASONAL CELEBRATIONS

For our industry, Christmas is usually the busiest time of the year. Things get out of control and people become more stressed. This makes it the perfect time to bring in some extra joy, happiness and spirit into the workplace!

Apart from Christmas being a fun and festive holiday, it can also add many benefits to your workplace as a whole. By taking part in Christmas and celebrating with your colleagues, you create an opportunity to boost morale in the office and teams, and bring everyone together. This will lighten the mood overall.

There are many different ways you can bring the Christmas spirit into the office. Some of the things we like to do at Future Fitouts are outlined below.

Keep in mind that it is your responsibility to ensure that everyone in your office is comfortable with Christmas being celebrated, and that they can come to you with any concerns.

DECORATE THE OFFICE

Decorating the office is one of the most simple and cheap ways to get into the Christmas spirit.

Distribute baubles around the office to bring in some sparkle and cheer. Place them in small corners that might be overlooked, like book shelves, and hang them from the ceiling.

Use tinsel to line desks, stairs, doorways, poles, handrails, or the perimeter of any room. Tinsel is an impactful and cost effective alternative when decorating your office.

Fill your space with ornamental reindeer, Santa Clauses, gingerbread houses and everything else Christmas! Get creative and consider the style of ornaments you would like to incorporate. You could even use just your branding colours. If your office looks high-end, sleek and sophisticated ornaments will more likely suit.

Christmas tree and wreath

Not only will a Christmas tree give your space that instant festive feel, putting it up as a team will give your staff an opportunity to bond doing something fun. If your office decides to do Secret Santa, the Christmas tree could also be a place where everyone places their gifts!

Putting up a wreath on the door is a great way to spread holiday cheer before anyone has even entered your space. It is an unspoken invitation that suggests Christmas cheer is welcome in your office!

Twelve days of Christmas

This is a great idea that can also serve as a countdown until your office shuts up shop for the year. Each day for 12 days, give your staff a small gift. Some ideas include a tray of mangoes, a scratchie, a tin food donation to a local charity, ice creams in the freezer, popcorn afternoon, or two hours off for Christmas shopping.

OTHER DAYS TO CELEBRATE

Keep in mind that not everybody celebrates Christmas, and some people may have their own religious or seasonal celebrations that they like to take part in throughout the year. It is important to observe and celebrate these events to show your staff that their beliefs and customs are valued and important.

I love our multicultural team at Future Fitouts. In the office we celebrate Diwali, Ramadan, and Independence Day, just to name a few.

Become That 1% Business

This section is very special to me. It compiles some of the most valuable lessons and advice that Aaron and I have been gifted over the years. Advice from our very first business coach (who we engaged on Valentine's day, only six weeks after meeting each other) to various consultants, as well as lessons we have taught ourselves over the years.

Some of the advice on this list might seem 'small'. However, it is usually the little things that make a big impact on your business and allow you to stand out and be that 1% company.

Your advisors are your best friends.
I'm not saying that your best friend should be advising you on business, but you need to be surrounded by the right team, who can be trusted to put your company's best interests first. Being at the top of a business can be lonely. You want to feel supported by those around you so that you can go to them when you need help or advice.

Be grateful and have a positive mindset.
Always see the positive! Opportunity is everywhere, you just have to look. Once you commit to having a positive mindset, great things will come your way.

Cheapest is not always best.
Sometimes, you need to spend money to make money. When you cut corners trying to save a couple of dollars here and there, it usually just results in you having to spend more money further down the track. This is true in almost every aspect of business. When you do the research and pay for quality, quality is what you will get.

Think differently!
If you are ever going to make a splash in the business world, you must think differently. Stand out from the competition by offering something the others don't. Never stop innovating and stay on top of trends and developments.

Who killed my business?
Always plan for the worst-case scenario! You don't want your business to

collapse before your eyes over something that could have been prevented. Continually look to the future so that you don't become irrelevant or obsolete. You don't want to be a Blockbuster or Yellow Cabs!

Look after yourself!
Your health is your wealth! There is no point running yourself into the ground trying to do the impossible. Give yourself enough time for adequate sleep, exercise and nutrition. You need to stay healthy and strong so that you can perform your best for your business. After all, who will be able to run things if you are out sick?

Be the culture you want.
Culture is formed from the top down! Set a leading example by embodying the values you want to instil in your team and office.

Hire people smarter than you.
When you hire people who are smarter than you, your business will be more likely to succeed. They will be able to solve problems quickly, work independently, and may even be able to suggest valuable changes to your company that you might not have even known were needed. Give these people a reason to want to be a part of your company. Stand for something big and bring them on the journey.

Competitors don't exist, there is plenty of work to go around.
Though you should keep your finger on the pulse as to what services businesses similar to yours are offering, you don't need to continually stress about what your competitors are up to, how much money they are making, or how many clients they have. Instead, focus your energy on improving your business so that you can offer a premium service. The clients and cash will soon follow.

Use systems!
I've said it before and I'll say it again: **S**ave **Y**our **S**elf **T**ime **E**nergy, **M**oney and **S**tress. Systemise EVERYTHING!

Small fish are sweet; find your niche in a crowded space.
Your business will be more likely to succeed if your niche is focussed. Know your point of difference and use it to your advantage. When you own your niche, you can focus on doing it well. After all, it is better to be an expert in one thing, than mediocre at many.

Know your numbers and the value of a task.
Take the time to find out how much everything in your business costs, from materials to labour. Continually ask yourself, "Is this best value of my time?"

Invest in yourself.
An investment in education will pay off tenfold. Clients want to engage someone who knows their stuff, and employees want to work for someone who is an industry leader. Read up, attend courses and workshops, and engage a coach.

Take your clients on a journey.
When you show your clients that you care, you allow them to become part of the journey with you. Your clients' experience with your business must stand out. You want to be the one that everyone is talking about! Do what you can to remain in your clients' thoughts so that when they speak of you, they build your reputation. Never underestimate the power of word of mouth endorsements.

All it takes is doing something small, like sending a client a card on their birthday, to make them feel special and that they are more than just another paying customer. This is the point of difference in business. It is the small details that are often overlooked, but you should *never* underestimate them.

Prepare customised client proposals.
When preparing a client proposal, it is *crucial* that it is tailored to the recipient. There is no point giving a potential client a generic bid. You need the document to persuade the client as to why and how your business can meet their specific needs.

Staff first, clients second.
Think about it. If your staff aren't happy, how likely is it that they will offer clients their best service? Supporting staff should be the highest priority of

any business, for their wellbeing, but also for your company's performance. After all, the success of your business largely rides on your employees doing a good job.

Become award winning.
Say it out loud: "We are an award-winning company." Sounds good, doesn't it? Imagine being able to proudly say this sentence to your clients, boast it on your website, and market it on your socials.

When you become an award winner, you gain clout and credibility. Not only that, but business awards will often offer free publicity and networking for winners and sometimes even shortlisted applicants. This can be great exposure for your business.

> ❝ *Give back to the world at least what you have received."*
> *– Albert Einstein*

Giving Back

Being in business isn't all about making money and turning over profit. I believe you also have a responsibility to the community you operate in.

In helping your community, you can also reap rewards for your business. For example, by showing that you support and are involved in your local community, the members of that community are more likely to do business with you as they know your business is ethically minded.

Generally, companies want to do the right thing by their community and get involved. However, many don't know where to start!

So, how *do* you get involved?

SUPPORT A CHARITY
Knowing that your business is supporting a good cause helps give it more purpose. So, why not choose one or more charities that your business can donate to? You could even get your employees to collaborate on which charity your company should support.

There are a number of great organisations out there who can help your business make meaningful contributions to worthwhile causes. Buy1Give1 (B1G1) is a great example. B1G1 helps businesses generate measurable, long-lasting impacts with an easy to use system that allows a portion of every transaction to be given to a worthy cause.

The idea behind B1G1 is that every time a business sells something, they give something back. Businesses can easily do this by including a small donation with every product or service sold. (For example, for every copy of this book that is sold, Future Fitouts will make an impact with B1G1!)

When deciding on a charity to support, try picking a cause that is relevant to your business or industry. For example, a hospitality establishment might support a food drive, or a pet hotel could donate to an animal shelter.

VOLUNTEER

Many businesses organise social events so that their staff can bond and have fun together, but have you ever considered volunteering with your team? Not only will you be doing something meaningful for the community, your team will have the opportunity to build better connections with one another.

There are many corporate volunteering opportunities you can take advantage of. A quick Google search will bring up various options in your area. If you are unsure where to start, check out OzHarvest, CERES, RSPCA and Clean Up Australia.

TAKE PART IN A CHARITY EVENT

This could include attending, organising, or sponsoring an event. Think fun runs, high teas, charity balls, raffles and fundraisers.

If you don't have the resources to host a full event, auctioning or raffling off a few valuable donated items can be a great way to give back to a good cause. You could even host a community fundraiser to generate donations in the wider community.

Being part of a charity event can do wonders for your team's morale. If you choose to join a charity fun run, your whole team can get involved while also being encouraged to stay active. Alternatively, hosting a high tea will give your staff the opportunity to show off their creative baking skills while being social with colleagues.

SPONSOR A LOCAL CLUB OR SPORTING TEAM

A great way to directly support your community is to sponsor a local team or club. Many small sporting and creative clubs rely on the money provided by their sponsors to survive.

If you sponsor a sporting team, you will also get the added benefit of being able to advertise on the players' uniforms, the field during game play, or on the website, depending on your sponsorship agreement.

Sponsoring a local team will also generate positive word of mouth for your company. When a business sponsors a local sporting team, players and supporters see that sponsor as a friend and valuable member of the community.

MAKE CONSCIOUS BUSINESS DECISIONS

Businesses make decisions every day that have an impact on the local and global community, so it is important that you are conscious about the effect your choices have on the wider world. For example, stocking your business with environmentally friendly supplies or banking with an institution who invests their money ethically are simple ways you can help your community.

Even the smallest business decisions can make a big impact. For example, at Future Fitouts, we have made sure that even our toilet paper is ethical. We choose to purchase toilet paper from Who Gives A Crap, a company that makes their toilet paper from 100% recycled paper and donates 50% of their profits to building toilets for those in need.

FUTURE FITOUTS GIVES BACK

At Future Fitouts, we're big supporters of giving back to our community. As of 1 July 2017, Future Fitouts became a proud B1G1 business, making impacts around the world so that we can live true to our vision: changing the world by transforming spaces.

We regularly support local charities and participate in community fundraisers and events. We are also dedicated to partnering with small businesses to help them grow and thrive.

Every business has the ability to be part of the wider community, and we hope that your company will have the courage to give back and take on one of the above methods of support.

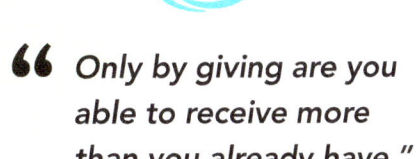

> 66 *Only by giving are you able to receive more than you already have."*
> *– Jim Rohn*

Never Give Up

Business is tough! I am *certainly* not going to say that I have it nailed. I'm sure I will face many more challenges during my business life! However, I know what a positive attitude and being surrounded by the right people can do.

When things get tough, keep your head high and never lose optimism. Opportunity is everywhere.

Still need some extra motivation? Look at these major companies who started out in their garages!

APPLE

Apple has changed the world and is one of the biggest and most well known brands today. However, that wasn't always the case.

In 1976, Apple's first computers were built in a small garage in Cupertion, California – the garage of Steve Jobs's adoptive parents to be exact. Steve Jobs, Steve Wozniak and their small team hand built 50 computers in 30 days, with the first sale being made to a local retailer for $500 a piece. A few decades later and Apple is now one of the biggest technology companies in the world.

GOOGLE

It might seem like Google dominates the internet today, but back in 1998 – when the value and potential of the internet was just being realised – Larry Page and Sergey Brin had only just thought up the idea for the online search engine. To turn this dream into a reality, they rented the garage at Susan Wojcicki's house in California to help pay her mortgage, and spent the next five months creating the search engine. Once it was up and running, they had already outgrown the garage and moved into an office. Google is now the world's biggest and most popular search engine.

AMAZON

Amazon is the biggest online store in the world, so it is easy to forget that this goliath only started as an online bookstore in 1994.

Amazon founder Jeff Bezos saw an untapped market for selling books online. He wanted to pursue it, so he gave up his high-flying career as vice president of a successful Wall Street investment firm and started the website from his garage in Washington. Because he operated out of a garage, his very first client meetings and contracts were negotiated and signed at the nearby Barnes and Noble.

MATTEL

The origin story of Mattel, one of the largest toy companies in the world, is truly inspiring. Company founders Harold 'Matt' Matson, Ruth Matson, and Elliot Handler were originally making picture frames from their garage in Southern California. Unfortunately for the trio, they were very quickly going broke.

In 1945, they began to make dollhouses out of picture frame scraps. After some time, the dollhouses began to outsell the picture frames. It didn't take long before their focus switched to manufacturing toys.

Mattel then soared to new heights in 1959 when Ruth invented the Barbie doll. Mattel is now one of the most popular and well known toy brands in the world.

DISNEY

Before the iconic Disney animated movies hit our screens, Walt Disney struggled to make his name in animation.

The very first Disney studio was set up in the Los Angeles garage of Walt Disney's uncle, where, in 1923, the very first Disney animated films were made. The short films created in this garage soon became inspiration for the original Alice in Wonderland animated movie.

The road towards success was a bumpy one for Walt Disney, but with passion and persistence he pushed through, and today Disney has become the highest grossing media conglomerate in the world.

Our Own Road to Success...

Whilst we are just a humble fitout company in Brisbane, Aaron *did* start the company in his garage, and then outgrew the home office equally as quick. Our first 'real' workspace that we leased was in an old industrial tin shed. We had just had a baby and were in desperate need to move out of the home office, but didn't have much money to spend on something nice.

The shed overheated in summer and was *freezing* in winter. Everything that could go wrong, did (I'm convinced it was cursed!). We had a high turnover of staff and continually attracted the wrong people into the business. The space was unattractive – a basic kitchenette tucked into a corner, leaking toilets – and vermin crawled through the cracks in the backdoor at night. It also backed onto a railway line and a busy road which made it incredibly noisy inside.

We knew the space was a stepping stone and that we could do better. Whenever we hired for a new role, we shared our dream of the 'new future office' and made sure that everyone knew the shed was only temporary. (We did this to try and attract the right team members, proving that staff are even subconsciously influenced by their work environment.)

In 2015, our office flooded in a freak disaster. An old hydrant water pipe in the street burst and shot high pressured water 15 metres into the air, taking with it debris and rocks that landed on the roof of our building and caused some of the pipework to break. The entire space was flooded in ankle deep water. We were all over the news and quickly realised that we had to make the move onto something better.

We found a new premises, commenced the fitout process, and moved. Fast forward a few years, and we were able to complete our dream 'Google inspired' office. The rest is history! It was undeniably tough, expensive and stressful, but we made it work, and are eternally glad that we did.

Office 1

Office 2

Office 3

Thank You from Lauren

Thank you from the bottom of my heart for taking the time to read *The Future of Business*. It was an absolute pleasure sharing my tips and tricks with you, and I hope you gained valuable and practical insight into both the fitout process and building and creating a successful business. I hope I have been able to convey ideas that you can implement in your own business.

Please make sure to take full advantage of the interactive feature of the book. It will increase your knowledge of design, fitout and culture and will help you come up with some of your own inspired and creative ideas.

We at Future Fitouts are experienced, knowledgeable and we care. If you would like to organise an appointment to discuss what we can do for you, please contact us through our contact form at www.futurefitouts.com.au or give us a call on 1300 368 461.

Lauren is sharing more in her INTERACTIVE book.

See exclusive videos, audios and photos.

DOWNLOAD it now at deanpublishing.com/futureofbusiness

Author Book Recommendations

- Breathe (James Nestor)
- Culture is Everything (Tristan White)
- The Accidental Entrepreneur (Janine Allis)
- The Leadership Contract (Vince Molinaro)
- Atomic Habits (James Clear)
- Extreme Ownership (Jocko Willink and Leif Babin)
- Chapter One (Daniel Flynn)
- The 7 Habits of Highly Effective People (Stephen R Covey)
- Rich Dad, Poor Dad (Robert T Kiyosaki)
- The Magic of Thinking Big (David J. Schwartz)
- The Compound Effect (Darren Hardy)
- The Slight Edge (Jeff Olson)
- Better Business, Better Life, Better World (Paul Dunn, Masami Sato, Daniel Flynn, Bernadette Jiwa, Yanik Silver and many more)

Permissions

Excerpt about Commercial Property Depreciation on Page 43. Permission from BMT Tax Depreciation, content from Bradley Beer, CEO.

Excerpt about Love Languages on Page 214. Permission from Moody Publishers, *The 5 Languages of Appreciation in the Workplace: Empowering Organizations by Encouraging People*, by authors Gary Chapman and Paul White, (2019).

Excerpt about Gong Sound Meditation on Page 222. Permission from Gong Sound Meditation, 'How a gong sound meditation benefits your corporate wellness program', by author Leith James, (2016).

Acknowledgements

This book would not have been possible without a number of special people in my life – past, present and future!

Firstly, a heartfelt thank you to my parents for providing me with the most precious gift of all: LIFE! Thank you from the bottom of my heart for your unwavering support, unconditional love, and down to earth upbringing filled with lifelong lessons. You have encouraged me to chase my dreams and believed in me every step of the way – I will be forever grateful.

To my sister and brother-in-law – I am grateful to have you in my life and for our close bond and friendship that has deepened over the years. Also, thank you for making me a proud Aunty!

To my grandparents, Nana and Pop. I have so many fond memories and experiences that I will treasure for my lifetime. I love you both dearly and admire your passion for life, good health, and young-at-heart positive attitudes. I will be forever grateful for the special relationship we have always shared.

Of course, my beautiful, strong, independent, and confident daughter Eva. Every day you make us proud. You are a blessing and have enriched my life like I could never have imagined. You are my biggest teacher and wise beyond your years. I know that you will go on to do great things, and my wish for you is, and always will, be: love, health, and happiness. May all your dreams come true, darling girl. I will always love you more!

My husband, Aaron. None of this would have been possible without you. I know it hasn't always been smooth sailing, but our challenges have only made us stronger. You are my partner in life and business – in your words, "we do everything together." I wouldn't have it any other way and I am grateful that I have been able to build a life and business (from nothing) with my best friend. Thank you for supporting me while writing this book. I love you.

To my mentors, teachers, advisors, and coaches from far and wide, I thank you for every word of advice, every conversation, every tear, every fear, and every triumph that I have shared with you. Thank you for your wisdom, your lessons, and for pushing me outside of my comfort zone (even when I have resisted). You all know who you are! A special thank you to the many of you who have been part of the FF Journey since the beginning.

My high school English teacher, for believing in me from a young age. This is one assignment you haven't had to proofread for me!

My circle of friends for understanding why I can't always make social commitments, for always lending an ear to listen and a shoulder to cry on, and for just accepting me for who I am.

To my extended family members for being a part of my life in some way, shape, or form and celebrating my achievements along the way.

The team at Dean Publishing! We got there!! What an extraordinary journey I've been on with you all. It's been a pleasure working with each of you. Thank you for bringing this book to life – literally!

And finally, cheers to all the challenges, setbacks, sleepless nights, and stress – thank you for building my character and proving that anything is possible!

" Difficult roads often lead to beautiful destinations. The best is yet to come"
– Zig Ziglar

Testimonials

This book is a must read for anyone striving to be a better leader, manager, or business owner. Teaching us how to deploy strategies and solutions into the workplace for all businesses (not limited to Fitout companies), Lauren provides excellent guidance that can be used on a daily basis to reinvigorate culture and success amongst all team members.

I have personally worked with Lauren for many years and watched the utilisation of these strategies in the creation of her multi-million dollar business, along with her husband Aaron.

Lauren has a passion for people, systems, and leadership. She has time and again successfully created a positive, reciprocal culture for team members, thus allowing coming to work to become an enrichment opportunity for all involved.

Lizzie Nelson, Director
Insurance Mentor Pty Ltd
Insurance Mentor is one of the largest Insurance Brokerages on the Gold Coast. Run by Lizzie Nelson and her business partner, Insurance Mentor utilises many of the strategies taught in The Future of Business *to ensure a positive team culture is solidified on a daily basis.*

Lauren has a depth of experience in creating great workplace culture and providing the right environment for teams to thrive. Lauren shares her insights into building an environment that promotes amazing teams and allows you to harness their potential.

Justin Hogg, Founding Director
Right Source Pty Ltd
With a strong focus on supporting social purpose by specialising in the Not-For-Profit, NDIS and Allied Health Sectors, Right Source provides a comprehensive accounting solution to any business that focusses on the people involved, as much as it does the numbers.

Highly recommend this book! Lauren has a strong drive and passion for implementing systems, leadership, and culture and shares her knowledge and lessons throughout her book. *The Future of Business* is easy to read, and most importantly, allows business owners to implement 'quick wins' into their business without spending a lot of money.

The Future Fitouts team carried out the fitout of our current office, and the positive impacts the space has had on our team and business growth is profound. Two years later and we are still receiving positive feedback from everyone who comes in for a meeting. Highly recommend!

Lucas Meadowcroft, Co-founder/CEO
CROFTI & Tribu

CROFTI is an innovation strategy consulting business that empowers everyday businesses by supporting their IT service requirements. As an added extension to this service, Tribu was created by the same team and is a world-first SAAS platform developed to automate IT support by using Artificial Intelligence, built for Managed Service Providers (MSP's) by MSP's. Working with businesses everyday, both CROFTI and Tribu understand the importance of setting up the right environment and culture to build a high performing company!

This book is a must read for anyone striving to be a better leader and business owner. Lauren is passionate about order, systems, and culture. She knows that people are the greatest asset of a business, and the strategies she discusses are a direct reflection of what she and her husband Aaron continue to implement in their successful business.

Faye Caughey, Founding Partner
Kaibizzen
Business Clarity Mentor

Our world has changed. Forever. And that means that our businesses need a new story. And we need it now.

In this book you'll read a great story. Use it to create your own great new story. One that recognises that we're all at our very best when we are giving. One that recognises that your business story really can change lives — and not just the lives of your team, your suppliers and your customers but the lives of people you most likely will never meet.

Lauren has made that central to the way she does business. Her story, as you'll see, is one that attracts great customers and great team members too.

It's a story of purpose — a story of focusing on something bigger than yourself. And that becomes your very own never-ending story.

Enjoy creating it. Enjoy living it every moment too.

Paul Dunn, Co-founder and chairman
B1G1 (www.b1g1.com)

ENDNOTES

Introduction

1   Annex Media 'Future Fitouts' Industry Leaders, season 8, Foxtel, Australia

Part One

1   Campbell, Leigh (19 October 2017) 'We've Broken Down Your Entire Life Into Years Spent Doing Tasks', HuffPost Australia, accessed 22 February 2021.

2   Tristan White (2017) *Culture is Everything: The Story and System Of A Start-Up That Became Australia's Best Place To Work*, Advantage, Charleston.

3   Janine Allis (2020) The Accidental Entrepreneur, 3rd edn, John Wiley & Sons Australia, Milton.

4   Stan Phelps (2014) Cracking Into Google: 15 Reasons Why More Than 2 Million People Apply Each Year, Forbes, accessed 7 May 2021.

5   Tristan White (2017) Culture is Everything: The Story and System Of A Start-Up That Became Australia's Best Place To Work, Advantage, Charleston.

Part Two

1   Green Furniture Hub (n.d.) *Green Furniture Hub: We Choose to Reuse*, accessed 11 May 2021.

2   Planet Ark (n.d.) *Business Recycling: Planet Ark*, accessed 11 May 2021.

Part Three

1   Chris Bailey (2013) The exact color to paint your office to become the most productive, A Life of Productivity website, accessed 1 March 2021.

2   Erin Largo-Wright, W William Chen, Virginia Dodd and Robert Weller (2011) 'Healthy Workplaces: The Effects of Nature Contact at Work on Employee Stress and Health', *Public Health Reports*. https://doi.org/10.1177/00333549111260S116

3   A Craig, F Torpy, J Brennan and M D Burchett (2010) 'The Positive Effects on Office Plants', *Nursery Papers Technical*, accessed 12 May 2021

4   Joel S Warm and William N Dember (1991) 'Effects of olfactory stimulation on performance and stress in a visual sustained attention task'. *Journal of the Society of Cosmetic Chemists*

5   American College of Healthcare Sciences (16 September 2016) *5 Delightful and Work-Enhancing Essential Oils for the Office*, ACHS website, accessed 26 February 2021.

6   Mark Moss, Jenny Cook, Keith A Wesnes and Paul Duckett (2003). 'Aromas of rosemary and lavender essential oils differentially affect cognition and mood in healthy adults'. *International Journal of Neuroscience* DOI: 10.1080/00207450390161903

7   Green Furniture Hub (n.d.) *Green Furniture Hub: We Choose to Reuse*, accessed 11 May 2021

8   Terry S Friedmann (n.d.) *Attention Deficit Hyperactivity Disorder (ADHD) [PDF 176KB]*, accessed 26 February 2021.

9   Daiki Jimbo, Yuki Kimura, Miyako Taniguchi, Masashi Inoue and Katsuya Urakami (2009). 'Effect of aromatherapy on patients with Alzheimer's disease'. *Psychogeriatrics* dio:10.1111/j.1479-8301.2009.00299.x

10 Evonne Roman (31 July 2015) *Increasing Productivity: How Dual Monitors Can Save You Time and Money,* business.com, accessed 12 May 2021.

Part Four

1 McDonald's (n.d) FAQ's: How long does it take to cook a burger on the grill?, McDonald's website, accessed 3 June 2021.

2 Bob Thompson (11 January 2006) Bob Thompson interviews Jan Carlzon: What Business Leaders Can Learn From "Moments of Truth" [interview transcript], Customer Think, accessed 11 May 2021.

3 Rebecca Cassells (2017) 'happy workers: How satisfied are Australians at work?', Curtin University & mwah, Perth.

4 Household, Income and Labour Dynamics in Australia (HILDA) Survey, Wave 15

5 Rebecca Cassells (2017) 'happy workers: How satisfied are Australians at work?', Curtin University & mwah, Perth, 29.

6 Ibid, 28.

7 Abraham Maslow (1943) 'A Theory of Human Motivation', Psychological Review, 50(4):370-396.

8 Teresa M Amabile and Steven J Kramer (2011) 'The Power of Small Wins', Harvard Business Review, 89(5).

9 Patrick Bet-David (12 November 2019) 'A bad employee costs you 3-5 times their salary…' [Tweet], Patrick Bet-David, accessed 11 May 2021.

Part Five

1 William Marston (2014) *Emotions of Normal People*, Routledge, Taylor & Francis, United Kingdom.

2 DiSC Profile (n.d.) *What is DiSC?* DP website, accessed 11 May 2021.

3 DiSC Profile (n.d.) *DiSC Styles* DP website, accessed 11 May 2021.

4 Jobvite (2018) 2018 Job Seeker Nation Study: Researching the Candidate-Recruiter Relationship [PDF 2MB], accessed 10 May 2021.

5 Tony Robbins (6 January 2016) Tony Robbins interviews Eben Pagan: How To Hire Superstars [interview video file], YouTube, accessed 10 May 2021.

Part Six

1 Bruce W Tuckman (1965) 'Developmental Sequence in Small Groups', Psychological Bulletin, 63(6): 384-399 https://doi.org/10.1037/h0022100

2 Carol Wilson (2017) Bruce Tuckman's Team Development Model [PDF 281KB], Culture At Work, accessed 13 May 2021.

3 Ibid.

4 Daiki Jimbo, Yuki Kimura, Miyako Taniguchi, Masashi Inoue and Katsuya Urakami (2009). 'Effect of aromatherapy on patients with Alzheimer's disease'. *Psychogeriatrics* dio:10.1111/j.1479-8301.2009.00299.x

5 Bruce W Tuckman and Mary Ann C Jensen (1977) 'Stages of Small-Group Development Revisited', Group and Organization Studies, 2(4): 419-427.

6 Gary Chapman (2015) *The 5 Love Languages: The Secret to Love that Lasts*, Northfield

Publishing, Chicago.

7   Gary Chapman and Paul White (2019) *The 5 Languages of Appreciation in the Workplace: Empowering Organizations by Encouraging People*, Moody Publishers, Chicago.

8   Glassdoor (2017) Statistical Reference Guide for Recruiters: 50 HR and Recruiting Statistics for 2017 [PDF 2.5MB], Glassdoor, accessed 10 May 2021.

9   Leith James (2016) How a Gong Sound Meditation benefits your corporate wellness program, Gong Sound Meditation website, accessed 15 June 2021.

www.ingramcontent.com/pod-product-compliance
Lightning Source LLC
Chambersburg PA
CBHW041956080526
44588CB00021B/2762